I DOS

and

I DON'TS

of

MARRIAGE

MARCUS ROGERS

ISBN 978-1-64458-710-2 (paperback)
ISBN 978-1-64458-711-9 (digital)

Christian Faith Publishing, Inc.
832 Park Avenue
Meadville, PA 16335
www.christianfaithpublishing.com

Printed in the United States of America

If you find a King keep him. If you find a Queen protect her.
Don't try to reshuffle the deck, because you
might end up pulling a joker.

—Unknown

CHAPTER 1

We Go Together, But Do We Grow Together?

I want to hold your hand when we are eighty,
look back and say we made it, we overcame, we beat the
odds, we loved through it all. We built a legacy of love.
Loving God, loving each other, and loving people.

In elementary school, I remember young boy's passing notes to girls asking the question would you go with me? Pretty much asking would you like to be my girl? There would be a yes and a no box for them to check their answer in. It is easy to go with someone, but can you grow with someone? Sadly enough, many people still jump into relationships and marriage with this kind of mindset. There are some questions that you should ask yourself and that potential partner before you even consider any kind of relationship with them. Jumping into a relationship is easy, but it is not always easy getting out. You might go into a relationship as a blank piece of paper, it is guaranteed that you will come out on the other side marked up. Relationships leave marks that can be good or bad. There are consequences to give people pens to mark on the page that is your life. You could actually get into a relationship and leave it with less than what you came into it with. In some cases what is stolen from you is so severe; it is like a spiritual, emotional, grand larceny! You want to be in a relationship where you are adding to each other in a positive way, and not tearing each other down. You want to have a partner where you guys have a plan, and you're not just going together and rolling with whatever comes along but growing together despite all odds. You want to help each other become everything God has created you to be individually and as a team.

Marriage is about two halves coming together and becoming one. This relationship is not a boss to a worker, or a master to a slave, marriage is a partnership between two people. This partnership like any major corporation will produce a product. Depending on the chemistry of the partners, the product that comes forth can either be good or bad. When a company produces something, if the product is good they benefit from it, but if the product tanks they are affected by the aftermath. A smart inventor knows that he cannot just look at the outside of a corporation and say this building and this CEO look nice, I would like to partner with you to produce my product. You are going to want to step inside that building and see the facilities. You are going to want to see the CEOs work history and previous experiences with other products they have produced and marketed.

You can have a great product, but if you partner with the wrong person it could destroy your products potential. If you partner with a thief, they will steal your idea or cheat you out of income. If you partner with someone who is lazy, the product will never get off the ground or reach as many people as it possibly could. If you partner with someone negative, as soon as you hit a problem, or a rough season, they will discourage you and try to talk you into giving up. You also don't want to partner with somebody who does not know what they are doing or does not line up with your vision. You don't want to take your new computer idea to a dog food factory! They may have some resources, but probably don't have the connections and experience that will get your product the attention it needs.

People usually look for partners because they can't do something on their own. You may have some great ideas, dreams, and inventions, but only have half of what it takes to get it off the ground. It would be wise to take your invention to someone who has the capabilities to produce, advertise, and help get your product off the ground. There may be some things that you are weak in, but your partner can fill the void by being strong or more experienced in that area. Am I saying your relationship or marriage should be about what the other person can do for you? No, what I am saying is marriage is a partnership, and you should find someone who when you partner with them you both benefit from the relationship.

You both should make each other better and help each other reach their next level. If you partner with someone who is moving in a different direction than you, they will be busy focusing on their goals, and you will be trying to give your dream CPR. You will have two people coexisting as two halves working separately. When this happens, usually one person in the relationship is going to suffer, quit, or become bitter. Eventually for the marriage to work, the other person will have to sacrifice what they want, who they are, or their dreams to support the other partner. When two halves come together with a common goal, you have twice the strength and manpower and twice the chance of success.

When you get into a relationship, it is not enough to look at the outside and assume everything is good to go. You must know who you are, what your dreams are, what you want out of life, and a general idea of the direction you want to go. I am not saying two people can't be married and have separate dreams. I am saying if your dreams and goals in life cause you to be constantly pulled in separate directions, arguing, being stressed, trying to change each other, and belittling one another as opposed to working toward a goal as one unit, the likelihood of both of you reaching your dreams does not look good.

Your marriage will be like a tree. You both must have the same root system. Do you share the same values? If you love God, and your partner loves the things of this world, your root system will be weak. Whenever a storm comes, your tree will easily be blown over or take serious damage. Also, if you guys are not rooted in good ground, you will not produce good fruit. If one of you is happy, and the other one is bitter, the bitterness will poison the fruit the tree produces. Is your partner or yourself rooted in bitterness or unforgiveness from the past? If one of you feels free, but the other one feels smothered and is desperate for air, the tree will wither and die from lack of oxygen. There are people depending on the fruit your marriage produces.

You may have children, siblings, friends, coworkers, or other church members who are exposed to the fruit your marriage produces. You can poison your children by producing bitter, or bad fruit. You can put a bad taste in your sibling's mouths about marriage by always speaking badly of your marriage or allowing them to see the strife. You can turn people away from Jesus because they see a chaotic marriage and take your relationship as a representation of Christianity. This is why it is very important when choosing the person you marry. Some people are married for years without ever producing any good fruit. Some people never recover from a marriage that was chopped down and destroyed. You cannot not take this choice lightly or jump into it without much prayer.

A marriage is a union of two people becoming one. There are several things you should ask yourself before you choose to become one with someone. Often times, if you ask yourself many of the things we will discuss in this book, you will save yourself from wasting time on bad relationships. You will be able to identify right away that there is no point in dating certain individuals because your puzzle pieces just don't fit. They don't line up with the direction God is taking your life. Many people try to force them to fit, and that is why the divorce right has become so high. Here are a few things you should ask yourself.

Do you know who you are as an individual? Do you have a general idea of what your life goals are, and the direction your future is headed? Do you have a clue on what Gods plan is for your life? If the answer to these questions is no, you may not be ready for marriage just yet. One of the biggest problems in marriages today is that people often try to find themselves during the marriage or they wake up one day realizing they got married for all the wrong reasons, and now they are unhappy. The truth is that many people in today's day and age get married or start relationships for all the wrong reasons. They don't really understand the purpose and value of sex and marriage, and they abuse it for several reasons.

People often get married because the sex they had outside of marriage resulted with someone getting pregnant. Because they used something God designed for marriage, outside of marriage, and it produced a child, they feel the right thing to do would be get married. Some people get married because they are lonely. They are tired of being home alone. They don't use their free time to their advantage. Instead of focusing on how they could make best use of this time being single, they focus on how lonely they feel. Some individuals are looking for someone to save them from their mess. They may have had a bad relationship before, or financial trouble.

They may be facing some kind of situation that just seems too big for them, and they see marriage as some sort of salvation from their problems. Many young women spend their whole lives fantasying about their big day! They like the idea of having a wedding and having all eyes on them as they walk down the aisle in their white dress. They like the idea of all the glitz, glamour, and romance of a wedding ceremony. They imagine the proposal and the ring being placed on their finger without thinking about the responsibility that has also been placed on them. They spend most of their life being infatuated with the idea of a wedding without ever considering what it means to be a wife. Once they get married, they find out being a wife is not that easy. Many people are running from something.

They are looking to escape their home or reality of their life; they are looking for a rebound from a previous failed marriage. Some young girls may have grown up in bad home life situations, and marriage was their way out of that bad environment. Some men may have just gone through a divorce, and they fear not having someone in the home to do all the things their previous wife did. Some people are running from thoughts in their mind. They are the only one out of their friends who is still single and their mind is telling them they are getting too old. Others are consumed with lustful thinking they can't control, or they want to be validated through sex, but they want to have sex the "right way," so they jump into marriage.

Some people lose patience waiting for someone, and sometimes because their self-esteem was so low, they took the first offer that came along because they thought this may be their only chance. These are all very bad reasons to jump into a marriage. When you use marriage as a Band-Aid or a quick fix, it is always sure to be disastrous God didn't create marriage to be a Band-Aid, He created it to be a beneficial and powerful union between a man and a woman! Most people who jump into marriage without considering any of the things we talked about when considering partnership, usually wake up one day feeling miserable, or trapped in their marriage, wondering what else is out there for them.

You don't want to jump into something because it looked good, in a time where everything in your life was looking bad. This is like going to the grocery store when you are hungry, and you overspend shopping for your current appetite. If you had just let the feeling of hunger past, you would realize you didn't need all of the stuff you bought in that moment. You may even get home after shopping while hungry and realize you don't even want half of the stuff you bought. It is the same thing with marriage. That partner you got involved with may have only looked good at the time because you were so hungry you become impatient. When we are led by these feelings, and we ignore biblical principles, we often compromise and make bad choices that have long-term consequences and head toward disaster.

Now notice I didn't say end in disaster. I want to point that out because there is nothing that is too messed up or broken for God to fix. If you are in a bad marriage, it is possible for God to make it a good one. If you are separated, or pending divorce, it is possible for God to restore your marriage. If you're in a marriage that you feel alone, and your needs are not being met, it is possible for God to work on that individual and change them for the better and give you're a more fulfilling marriage! Maybe you did all of the things I just said not to do, and you are already married. Do not be discouraged and close this book. We serve a God who can turn around the impossible. He can do what no marriage counselor can do. He can save something that is drowning that the coast guard would have given up on! What limits man does not limit God. When we project the limits of our mind unto God, that is like putting handcuffs on God preventing Him from working. The Bible says without faith it is impossible to please God, and if we have the faith of a mustard seed we can look at a mountain and tell it to be removed. Is your marriage facing a huge mountain? The Bible says that God honors marriage, and He hates divorce. Don't give up just yet, if you put your marriage in Gods hand, because He honors it, it is very possible that your marriage will experience a life-changing miracle.

> For I hate divorce," says the Lord, the God of Israel, "and [c]him who covers his garment with wrong," says the Lord of hosts. "So take heed to your spirit, that you do not deal treacherously." (Mal. 2:16, NASB)

The earliest use of the English word, "marriage," dates back to the 13th century, but the concept of marriage comes from God. Marriage by God's design is the union of one man and one woman (Gen. 2:18). Some say that it is the ceremony or wedding that makes the man and woman married; God's word tells us that it is the joining of flesh that makes the marriage (Gen. 2:24). Becoming one flesh with someone is very important. Whatever they have, you become one with it. Whatever is in their spirit, their mind, their heart, can attach itself to you. Many times, people get in relationships and marriages and adapt to who the other person is. You may have seen someone you know get involved or married to someone, and later on down the road they seem like a completely different person. They start acting different, they get involved in things that you never thought would have interested them before, and it is almost impossible to recognize them. When you get with someone either you flow in unity, change yourself to adapt to the other person, or bump heads until it ends in separation. The Bible says, "Can two people walk together without agreeing on the direction?" (Amos 3:3, NLT).

When you join flesh, you are either going to embrace that oneness or your spirit is going to treat it like your body would an infection and you wind up rejecting it or becoming sick the longer you are exposed to it. When you become one with somebody, you take on a part of them for the rest of your life, good or bad. This does not just happen sexually. You have to be careful what you expose yourself to. Everybody's way of thinking, or influence on you is not always healthy, nor is it always right. By exposing yourself to certain kinds of people, it could leave damage on you that changes the way you look at life, and every future relationship. A few bad choices in relationships can leave you in a state of disability. You become a handicap and don't realize it until you finally settle down with the person you want to spend the rest of your life with. Now all those bad things and patterns of thinking you took on from past relationships leave your new relationship in a state of dysfunction and disability because you are unable to operate at 100 percent.

You become like an injured war veteran. Have you ever see those guys who lose a leg or a Vietnam veteran in a wheel chair? This is how you look emotionally and spiritually inside through the wars of bad relationships. Because of the wounds you took in a past relationship, you are unable to fully walk and run in your final one. You try to trust, but you are limping. You try to love, but you are bleeding. You try to be open, but your so bandaged up you are closed off like a mummy. Because of lies, bitterness, resentment, memories of pain, you are unable to love your spouse fully as God created you to do. You are unable to experience the beauty and companionship that could be found in your marriage the way God desires it to be. Instead of you becoming one with the person God created for you, you guys become spiritually schizophrenic.

You take on everything you become one with in your past, which stole a part of who you are away, and become one with whatever that person brings to the union as well. When you give yourself to the wrong people, they take something away from you that didn't belong to them, and they inflict wounds on you, that you should have never received. This takes away from the beauty, and power of the union God designed for you to have. In later chapters, I will talk about soul ties and displaced anger. These things could be preventing you from having your best marriage now!

Because of everything I mentioned, this is why it is so important to understand who you are as a person, and the importance of sex and marriage before you just jump into it. There is more to it than just hoping in the bed with someone. There is more to it than just having a ceremony and saying I do. You do not just jump into any of these things without taking on some baggage you didn't come with.

The world will try to tell you otherwise, but it can never escape Gods ultimate design for either. There is a purpose for sex and marriage in God's eyes. When we understand this, we get a new perspective on how we value these things. We learn to treat it with more respect, and appreciate it in a way that would be pleasing in Gods eyes. If you are thinking about marriage, or sex, I want you to really understand the importance of this convenient and vow before God.

Many people don't take vows serious anymore, but you must understand that you made a covenant with God. This is very important. Traditional marriage vows go something like this,

> I, Jennifer, take you, Jacob, to be my husband, to have and to hold from this day forward, for better, for worse, for richer, for poorer, in sickness and in health, to love and to cherish, until we are parted by death. This is my solemn vow.

Divorce is so popular nowadays. As soon as something isn't going good, people give up, abandon, or cheat on their marriage. You have to take this vow you made before God very serious. God is the creator of marriage, and from the dawn of time He established that it would be one man joined to one woman.

> So the LORD God caused a deep sleep to fall upon the man, and while he slept took one of his ribs and closed up its place with flesh. And the rib that the LORD God had taken from the man he made into a woman and brought her to the man. Then the man said, "This at last is bone of my bones and flesh of my flesh; she shall be called Woman, because she was taken out of Man." Therefore a man shall leave his father and his mother and hold fast to his wife, and they shall become one flesh. And the man and his wife were both naked and were not ashamed. (Gen. 2:21–25)

This is such a powerful bond when you do it Gods way. God has a rib for every man. God has a home for every woman. Adam and Eve did not accidently meet up, it was by divine design. They didn't just meet up and have a one night stand or do Netflix and chill and engage in casual sex. If you read the whole story, God had a plan for everything, and nothing was by chance. Many people just go with whatever they feel in the moment without seeking out God's plan for their life. Many people abuse the union of sex outside of marriage and wonder why their life is out of order.

It was never God's design for Adam to run from woman to woman become one flesh with more than just Eve. God has a custom life partner designed for you, but there is a process you must go through before you are ready to enter into this union and covenant before God. Some young lady wonders why a guy keeps rejecting her and all of her effort, it is because you are not his rib. His body is rejecting you, and when you try to make it fit, that is like performing a heart transplant without having the matching blood types. The body will reject it and eventually die. God has a place for you, but there is a process that comes with that. You must understand God takes this covenant between a man and woman very serious.

> But you say, "Why does he not?" Because the LORD was witness between you and the wife of your youth, to whom you have been faithless, though she is your companion and your wife by covenant. (Mal. 2:14–15)

If you don't honor a contract, you make with men there are many consequences to that. Your credit score could take a hit, you could be sued, or even jailed. Marriage is a contract before God, and it is very important that you take this seriously. It is not something you can just jump in and out of whenever you feel like it. Many people don't take it as serious as they should because they never see the results of breeching that contract right away. We take people in the world more serious than we take God sometimes and that is a shame. Yes, He is a God of great mercy, and grace, but that does not mean we should not fear and respect Him. Many people don't experience the damage of breaking their covenant with God till sometime later down the road. They see the affects in their children, their pay, their dreams, their ministry, or they wake up realizing one day when it is too late, that they made the biggest mistake of their life.

As I mentioned before, many people jump into relationships and marriage before they know who they are. Many people use these things to try to discover who they are and that is why they bring on so much pain into their lives. Once they start discovering who they are, what they like, and what they want to do in life, their perspective on their marriage can change. Sometimes, when they start making changes in their life to pursue that new dream, hobby, or goal, they realize their partner may not be very supportive of the changes. Many times, they find themselves outgrowing their partner and find themselves no longer satisfied with the state or position of the marriage. One person may be content with life the way things are and is unwilling to change, support, or experience new things. They may not want to step out of their comfort zone, and many times, they may simply not have an interest in the things you have become interested in. This causes there to be great tension and conflict, and often, people feel like they are being held back. They want to take sail, but their partner becomes an anchor that is holding them back from exploring the oceans of life.

In the following chapters, I will show you the steps to follow to have the marriage God has designed for you. In the next chapter, I will start with the men, as God did in the book of Genesis. One of the first things a man needs to know, is who He is and what God expects from Him as a man. There is a process for this.

CHAPTER 2

You Can't Be A Real Man Without God, What Does God Expect of a Man?

Do not pray for easy lives. Pray to be stronger men.
—Reverend Phillips Brooks

Before we even talk about what God expects out of you as a husband, we must understand what God expects from you as a man. If you don't know how to be a Godly man, you will be taking on more than you can handle trying to be a husband. God has a process, and we must lay down the proper foundation in order to build future success.

If you look at the story of Adam in the book of Genesis, one of the first things God did was make man in His own image. This lets us know that God has always desired for man to be a reflection of who He is. The second thing we see is that before God gave Eve to Adam, He had already given Adam a job to do around the garden. If you look at the verse in Genesis chapter 2, you will see that God not only gave Adam a job, but He gave him instructions as well. He gave Adam the blueprint for success in his life. Every man must acknowledge God, and seek out instructions and directions for his life in order to blessed and victorious.

Before you even consider looking for a wife, you need to make sure your foundation is straight. There are a few things every man needs to have in hand to start building his life. The first thing is relationship with God. We see clearly that it was not a strange thing for God to speak with Adam in the garden. When you have a relationship with God, He will begin to give you instructions, boundaries, and goals for the direction of your life. We see that after Adam was created, God spoke to him and gave him directions, purpose, and a job to do. Adam was a man with relationship with God, a vision, a purpose, and a job before Eve ever came into the picture. God set Adam up for success.

If the man you are interested in does not have a blueprint in hand, that is a warning sign. If you are a man and you are reading this and saying, "I don't have a blueprint, I don't have directions, I don't know what I am doing or where I am going," then you also need to be saying, "I don't need to be looking for a woman either." God is a God of order. If you want to be blessed, let your moves be in order with God's will. Not saying you have to be all the way perfect or all the way together, but you need to have those two basic things to build a foundation. If you try to find a woman first, you are building backwards. If you find a woman, but don't have a vision, you might find out quick that the woman you thought was a good idea, doesn't line up with the vision God gave you.

As a man, the only way to access these things is through a real relationship with God. Often times we go through life and exclude God from our everyday life decisions. Many only come to God after they have made a mess of things. The Bible says acknowledge God in all of your ways, and He will direct your path. It clearly says all your ways, not some of your ways, or sometimes, but all of the time. God wants to be at the center of everything a man sets himself to do! We men must have the kind of relationship with God where we are willing to submit. If He tells us no, but our feelings say yes, we must be willing to live with the no. We cannot blame God, or say it is the devil, when it is simply are poor choices that are not authored by God that get us into a world of hurt.

> The LORD God took the man and put him in
> the Garden of Eden to work it and take care of it.

And the LORD God commanded the man, "You
are free to eat from any tree in the garden; but
you must not eat from the tree of the knowledge
of good and evil, for when you eat from it you
will certainly die." (Gen. 2:15)

God created man in His own image and gave us authority and
dominion over the earth from the very beginning. This means before
you have a wife, you need to have a job and be able to provide for
that wife. You also need to know who you are in this life and have
the ability to walk around with your God-given authority and know
how to use the dominion God gave you. You need to be able to work,
provide, protect, and be secure in who you are as a man before you
get blessed with a wife from God. God and Adam had a close relationship, and this is the key for every man. Your relationship with
God should be more serious than the one you pursue when you chase
a girl you really like.

When we are really into a girl and want her attention, we pursue her with kind words, dates, romance, flirting, our time and gifts.
You must pursue God with the same passion, faithfulness, and desire.
You shouldn't be surprised to hear from God, or receive directions
from Him. You shouldn't be confused about if you are hearing the
voice of God or not, and if you are unsure, you should be able to
see if what you hear matches up with God's word. You don't want
to have a causal relationship with Jesus. You don't want to treat Jesus
like some men treat a side chick, or a girl they are really not too
interested in. Jesus needs to be your first love. If you don't love God
and don't understand how God loves you, you can never understand
how to love and take care of a wife. If your relationship with God is
shaky, don't even consider marriage until you build something more
solid with God. If you can't lead yourself to God and be sure of His
direction, how can you expect to lead a woman, or for her to follow
you once she realizes you don't know what you're doing.

Then the man and his wife heard the sound of
the LORD God as he was walking in the gar-

den in the cool of the day, and they hid from
the LORD God among the trees of the garden.
(Gen. 3:8)

It was not uncommon for God to speak to Adam in the garden.
We see in the story that God would walk through the garden and talk
with Adam. Later on in Genesis, we see God speaking to Adam's son,
Cain, in an audible voice and that Cain was accustomed to this. It
was not like later on in the New Testament where Saul fell on his face
and was blinded when God spoke to him on the road to Damascus.
As a man, you need to be able to know you can go before God and
that He will hear and answer you. You must know that God does not
always tell us what we want to hear, but He tells us what we need to
know. You want to have a mature relationship with God before you
take on a wife or serious relationship. There are several reasons for
this.

In order for any man to know who he really is, he must have a
genuine relationship with Jesus. Many people go through life with a
mediocre relationship with God. They only pray or read their Bible
so they don't feel guilty. They only praise and worship when they
are at church in order to be seen. They only call God when they are
going through a hard time. They treat God more like a butler than a
friend, or Lord. There is no way for the plans of God to be revealed
to you for your life through casual Christian living. God wants to
be at the center of your life. He shaped and created us from dust,
and the Bible says that He knows the very number of hairs on our
head. He knows what is best for your life. He has better insight and
a better understanding of who you are and your purpose than you,
your mother, your father, your pastor, or anyone else. Many times,
we go through life trying to navigate whatever falls into our path or
following whatever feelings we have, and this is what causes us to fail.
God doesn't want you to follow your feelings. Every good idea isn't
a God idea.

"For I know the plans I have for you," declares
the LORD, "plans to prosper you and not to

harm you, plans to give you hope and a future."
(Jer. 29:11)

Trust in the Lord with all your heart, And lean
not on your own understanding; In all your ways
acknowledge Him, And He shall direct your
paths. (Prov. 3:5–6, NKJV)

The problem is people prefer to walk by sight and not by faith. Many of us think we have all the answers for our lives, or that we know what is best for us. We really think we know what kind of job we want, what kind of wife we need, and where we want to live, but we often fail to realize that many of these thoughts are influenced by outside sources.

Your parents, friends, life experiences, and living conditions can influence many of the thoughts you have and form many of the desires you have. You may think you need a certain type of wife just because of the way your mother treated you regardless of if it was good or bad. You may think you want a certain type of job because that was the only thing you were exposed to as a child. There are boundaries all around us that are self and man-made. There are many things you never experienced, or never even thought of, because you simply were not exposed to it. This is the beautiful thing about walking with the Lord! He will expose you to things you never could have imagined. He will take you to places you never thought you could go. He will smash down every boundary in your mind and expose you to a beautiful brand new horizon! I can tell you right now at eighteen, you don't know anything about life, and everything you were exposed to and taught as a child isn't always right. You need to understand that as much as you love and respect your parents, they were wrong about a few things and even the things they were right about might not blend well with the person you are interested in. You need to take time to grow in the Lord, and seek God for yourself.

Often times, we make mistakes, bad marriage, or job choices based off the boundaries that have been placed in our minds. You may have grown up in a home where you were verbally abused and told what you couldn't do, or what you couldn't be. You may have been exposed to some kind of dysfunction in your home, but because that is what you know and are used to, you long for it. People on the outside looking in can see that the way you do, respond, or think about some things is wrong, but because you never were exposed to what right looks like, you grow up and are attracted to what you thought was normal.

You don't break beyond that boundary because you think there is nothing wrong with it. You don't leave an abusive relationship because you believe that is something all marriages go through. You don't apply for college because somebody told you that you were too stupid. You sleep around with several women and take them for test drives, use them, or cheat on them because that is what your father did. Many people live in dysfunction their whole lives and don't even know it. They assume that this is just the way things are. Getting close to God will expose the dysfunction in your life. You want it to be exposed before you build a family, and pass that dysfunction into your marriage and unto your children.

It is time for you to go from dust to dominion. God shaped you and created you out of the dust with purpose. He put time and effort into making you the man or woman you are. Every gift, talent, and ability you have comes from God. Before people got to you and tarnished what God made, you were created with purpose. You were created with authority. We all come into life like a blank piece of paper, but best believe after you live a couple of years, you will have marks all over from the things and people you will be exposed to once you leave the protection of the womb.

Once Eve and Adam got exposed to the snake, their thought process began to change. It is the same thing with you and me! God created us with great plans for our lives, and He equipped us with everything we need to accomplish what He has for us, but many times, being exposed to imperfect people and imperfect situations tampers, clouds, and sometimes even destroys what God has designed for us. You have to guard your mind, your dream, and everything God has placed inside of you.

Imagine what God has placed inside of you as a seed. In order for that seed to take root and grow, it must be watered, exposed to light, and protected from critters. It must be planted and grounded! This is where relationship with Jesus comes into play. You must take your heart, your cares, your thoughts, your plans, your hurts, and everything else and place it into the hands of God. He can do more with it than you can! He sees things that you can't see, and He knows things that you don't know. Instead of struggling through life with the perspective of an earthworm, look up to God with the perspective of an eagle and let him guide you, and point out the dangers as you crawl along. Just know the process won't be easy. A seed is buried, and when the water hits it, it breaks. Sometimes, God will bury you and break you in order for you to grow!

> The Lord is my shepherd, I lack nothing. He makes me lie down in green pastures, he leads me beside quiet waters, he refreshes my soul. He guides me along the right paths for his name's sake. Even though I walk through the darkest valley I will fear no evil, for you are with me; your rod and your staff, they comfort me. You prepare a table before me in the presence of my enemies. You anoint my head with oil; my cup overflows. Surely your goodness and love will follow me all the days of my life, and I will dwell in the house of the Lord forever. (Pss. 23:1–6, NIV)

This is a very familiar scripture in the Bible, but many people never fully take the time to truly understand what this verse is saying. The Lord is our shepherd, He will lead us to green pastures and still waters. You wonder why life has you feeling sick? It is because you keep wandering off and eating dead grass. You follow your feelings and every aroma of sin that the enemy sends your way, and it causes you to be exposed to some bad things. You wonder why you feel like you are drowning in life? It is because you followed your own lust and tried to drink from some waters that were too dangerous or moving too fast for you and you fell in. You had no business being down at those waters in the first place, and if you had stayed closed to the Shepherd, He would have told you not to go play by that dead grass, poison ivy, or dangerous waters. If you allow the Lord to lead you, that does not mean that the wolves will never attack but when it's all said and done, you will be blessed. God never promised life will be easy, but He does promise to guide us through it.

If you let God lead you young men, He will lead you to the good wife, the good job, the green pastures. Many times, when we follow our own lust, we see some water that looks good, but when we stick our head in to take a drink, we find out that the current is moving way too fast for us. Everything you try to build gets swept away in that current and you find yourself in a hole deeper than where you started.

The Bible breaks it down quite simply for young men. You can't jump into a relationship just because she looks good on Instagram, or because she says sweet and encouraging words in your inbox. Women can be very manipulative, and if you are not staying close to God, you can fall into the arms of a Delilah and lose your blessing like Sampson. This is a long verse to read, but it is a very necessary one for any young man to read.

Avoid Immoral Women

"My son, pay attention to my wisdom; listen carefully to my wise counsel. Then you will show discernment, and your lips will express what you've learned. For the lips of an immoral woman are as sweet as honey, and her mouth is smoother than oil. But in the end she is as bitter as poison, as dangerous as a double-edged sword. Her feet go down to death; her steps lead straight to the grave. For she cares nothing about the path to life. She staggers down a crooked trail and doesn't realize it. So now, my sons, listen to me. Never stray from what I am about to say: Stay away from her! Don't go near the door of her house! If you do, you will lose your honor and will lose to merciless people all you have achieved. Strangers will consume your wealth, and someone else will enjoy the fruit of your labor. In the end you will groan in anguish when disease consumes your body. You will say, "How I hated discipline! If only I had not ignored all the warnings! Oh, why didn't I listen to my teachers? Why didn't I pay attention to my instructors? I have come to the brink of utter ruin, and now I must face public disgrace." Drink water from your own well— share your love only with your wife.[b] Why spill the water of your springs in the streets, having sex with just anyone? You should reserve it for yourselves. Never share it with strangers. Let your wife be a fountain of blessing for you. Rejoice in the wife of your youth. She is a loving deer, a graceful doe. Let her breasts satisfy you always. May you always be captivated by her love. Why be captivated, my son, by an immoral woman, or fondle the breasts of a promiscuous woman? For the Lord sees clearly what a man does, examining every path he takes An evil man is held captive by his own sins; they are ropes that catch and hold him. He will die for lack of self-control; he will be lost because of his great foolishness." (Prov. 5: 1–23, NLT)

God knows what the best path is for you young men. We may have ideas in our head or desires in our heart, but we must not walk by what we feel, we must learn to be led by the Spirit of God. Every day when you wake up, you should be asking God to order your steps. We see in the previous verse I shared that not following God's directions can end in disaster. When you follow your lust or your own thoughts without acknowledging God, you will always head down the wrong path. When you cross over into enemy territory, you are fair game for the enemy. You have given the enemy legal access to mess with your life. When you stay in the presence of God, you are covered and protected. You do not want to be like the prodigal son and leave your father's home based off pride or lustful desires. This is a recipe for destruction.

The worst thing a man can do is, through following his own desire, build a foundation and start a family that has to deal with the consequences of his failure to put God at the center of his choices. This can cause damage for generation after generations. Just like there are some diseases that can be passed on genetically or because of exposure from parent to child, the same can be done with the consequences of your choices. You don't want to make any moves that are not ordered by God. The Bible says, "The steps of a good man are ordered by the Lord: and he delighteth in his way" (Ps. 37:23, KJV).

If you want to be a good man, your steps must be ordered by the Lord. If you want to be a blessed man, and have a blessed family, and have the favor of God on your life, your steps must be ordered by the Lord. If you want to break out of the dysfunction of your past, and how you grew up, and have a new victorious life for you and your future family, your steps must be ordered by the Lord.

You can't know who you are if you don't know who God is. We are so imperfect and flawed because of what we are exposed to in this world. The only thing to counteract that is the presence of God. Young men should be seeking God at the start, middle, and end of every single day. When you seek God and read His word, it will read you back. Relationship with God will show you who you are. It will show you your weaknesses that you didn't even know where there. It will show you strength that you never knew you had. It will show you talents, desires, and dreams that you didn't even know existed. After God shows you who you are and what His plan is for your life, He will give you the directions and blueprint for how get to where He is trying to take you. He will lead you to the green grass and still waters. When you walk with God, you can never fail. Even when it seems like you are losing, you are still winning because the Bible says all things will work for the good of those who love Him and are called according to His purpose!

Work on your relationship with God and ask Him to show you what you need to work on every day. When you pray, ask God for is His plan for your life. If you put Him at the center of your choices, He will bless the moves you make, and because He loves you, He will make sure the moves you make are what is best for you. Sometimes, it may not feel like it, but you must have faith. You may have to let go of and reject something that may seem good for you but, unlike Eve and Adam, you can reject the fruit from the enemy and live in the blessings of God! People often thank God for the doors He opens, but you should also thank Him for the ones He shuts.

Matthew chapter 6 tells us not to worry in this life because if we walk with God, He will take care of us. You never have to be afraid of your needs or desires being met when you submit your life to Jesus. Just keep walking with God and stay in His presence no matter what is going on around you. The enemy will try to lure you out of the protection of God. He will try to call you to take a short cut and come off the path God has set before you, but be faithful and God will take care of you.

> Therefore I tell you, do not worry about your life, what you will eat or drink; or about your body, what you will wear. Is not life more than food, and the body more than clothes? Look at the birds of the air; they do not sow or reap or store away in barns, and yet your heavenly Father feeds them. Are you not much more valuable than they? Can any one of you by worrying add a single hour to your life? And why do you worry about clothes? See how the flowers of the field grow. They do not labor or spin. Yet I tell you that not even Solomon in all his splendor was dressed like one of these. If that is how God clothes the grass of the field, which is here today and tomorrow is thrown into the fire, will he not much more clothe you—you of little faith? So do not worry, saying, "What shall we eat?" or "What

shall we drink?" or "What shall we wear?" For the pagans run after all these things, and your heavenly Father knows that you need them. But seek first his kingdom and his righteousness, and all these things will be given to you as well. Therefore do not worry about tomorrow, for tomorrow will worry about itself. Each day has enough trouble of its own. (Matt. 6:25–34)

God expects a man to have a sincere relationship with Him. He expects a man to work and seek out God for direction with His everyday life choices. He expects a man to be able to trust Him, and be firm in His faith no matter what He is facing. He expects man to protect, provide, and lead. He expects a man to walk in the God given authority and power he has. He expects a man to have dominion not only over the enemy, but his problems, his life, and his family. In summary, if you are not a man, you can neither be a husband nor can you handle the blessings of God. A wife is a privilege, an honor, a treasure, and an amazing blessing from God, but all blessings come with responsibility. The responsibility is not always light, sometimes it can be hard, but God expects a man to carry that responsibility on his shoulders, through the waters and mountains of life by the grace and strength of Jesus Christ. God works in decency and order, and you must follow the steps of spiritual growth and evolution to receive the things God has for you and to arrive at the places He is trying to take you.

If you can't carry your cross, you can't carry a wife. Many guys think they have what it takes because they feel like they are the man, or the world has been telling them they are the man all their life. The Bible always says pride goes before a fall. The way the world sees a man and the way God sees a man are two completely different things. God is not concerned with the size of your muscles and how much you can lift, but the size of your heart and how much you can love. He is not concerned with you being the tallest, most handsome, or hardest guy around. He is concerned with you being humble, patient, sensitive to His spirit to follow his direction. A man who is full of himself has no room for God. A man without God has a destiny with destruction. God won't bless a man who can't follow Him with people he loves and cares about. He knows that since he created man as the head, wherever he leads, the people in his family and ministry will follow.

What qualifies a man to be a man in God's eyes has nothing to do with the qualifications the world has. You can be the shortest, most skinny man, but have the biggest heart. You will have the strength to forgive and endure things that the six foot six guy could never handle. True strength comes from the inside, and the supply comes from God. A real man is a praying man. A real man is a faithful man. A real man is a man after God's own heart.

David was overlooked by his father and his brothers. The prophet, Samuel, looked at the outward appearance of his brothers and assumed because of what he saw on the outside they were the ones God had called to be anointed to be king. But the Bible says in 1 Samuel 16:7 (NIV), "But the Lord said to Samuel, 'Do not consider his appearance or his height, for I have rejected him. The Lord does not look at the things people look at. People look at the outward appearance, but the Lord looks at the heart.'"

The most important choice you will make in your life is the woman you marry. She can either be a help mate or a hell mate. She will either build with you or tear everything down you set your hands to do. Let God choose for you.

As I close this chapter, you will see we stressed relationship with God over and over again. Young men you may not have had a good example of what a man, marriage, or husband is supposed to be. That is okay, do not be discouraged. No matter what you feel you are lacking, God can be the Father your father never was to you, and lead you into success. Lean not unto your own understanding, but in everything you do acknowledge Him with an open and empty heart, and He will lead you into victorious living!

CHAPTER 3

Put Your Bucket Away, Girl
What does God Require of a Woman?

Who can find a virtuous woman? for her price
is far above rubies.
— Proverbs 31:10–31, KJV

Ladies, do you know your worth? Don't allow yourself to be his sometime, halftime, downtime, or spare time. If he isn't willing to commit and give you his full time, he is a waste of your time. So many women got their focus on the wrong man. I always say fall in love with Jesus, and everything else will fall into place. God will take care of you if you surrender your will and your ways to Him, and trust Him to meet your needs. God has the best man for you ladies, but before that man comes in to your life, you attention needs to be on the Son of man. The greatest man to ever walk the earth. Jesus needs to be your first man. You need to give Him your full attention.

We live in a world where many women are trying to catch a man or their lives revolve around finding a man. In my opinion, it seems where we live in a world where many woman are taught that finding the right man will fix all of their problems, and if you get with a man and things don't work out, he wasn't the right man, or he was a weak man, or not a good man. My sisters, the first thing I want to say is Jesus is the first man you need to be looking for. Stop thinking a knight in shining armor is going to solve all of your problems. If my knight would come, I wouldn't be lonely. If my knight would come, he could provide for me. If my knight would come, I would feel complete.

All of these things you feel or things that Jesus can handle! Some women put all their worth and hope in finding the right man, instead of focusing on being the right woman. Are you prepared for what you are praying for? Because if you are not, you can meet the right man and things still go bad. Don't listen to the world's advice, ladies. The world will have women thinking it just takes finding the right man instead of being the right woman. The reason this is dangerous is because some woman will never take responsibility for their actions or their life, and they will always go from man to man thinking the next one is just going to be so right everything will just magically work out. God has a plan for men, but he also has a plan for woman as well. Don't follow the ways of the world when it comes to dealing with men.

It does not take much time to scroll through Instagram, Facebook, or other social media platforms seeing girls half-dressed or posing provocatively trying to get attention or catch a man's eye. Many men struggle with lust and are visual creatures and they fall for it. Men can be so foolish that they think because it looks good on the outside it must be good overall. Sex, nudity, curves, and being provocative gets major attention in this world.

The problem is it seems that these girls are getting all the attention and the good women get ignored. Many men want to go out and have their fun then find them a good girl to settle down with. Young men often chase sex, and their whole life is centered around sex. They go to the club, talk to women, browse social media, and are just consumed with looking for sex. This is why they chase up after woman being openly sexy, because they feel that this will give them easier access to sex. If a man does not have relationship with God, he will spend most of his young life chasing sex. Many young guys go out and run all over the place, and then when they get a little older they want to find them a nice girl. They didn't mind messing around with all the loose women, but they want a nice woman to marry. They rejected the Godly girl, to go after the women of the world, to satisfy their lust and desires. Ladies, you don't have to settle for leftovers. I am not saying that a man with a past will not be a good husband, but if you don't want to settle for that, you don't have to, and there is nothing wrong with that.

There are older men and young men who have a desire and love for the things of God. The center of their universe is not chasing after sex, but chasing after relationship with God. My sisters, you don't have to look at the world and feel like you will be forgotten or single forever. You don't have to feel like you need to compete with the woman of the world for the attention of the men of the world. The reality is carnal men will be attracted to that, not Godly men. If you are a woman of God, you don't want a carnal man, because a carnal man can't lead you into everything God has for you. So, just know, you don't need to advertise yourself to get a man. All you need to do is get lost in your relationship with Jesus. You want to get so lost in God that the only way a man could find his way to your heart is if God gave him the directions.

You must protect yourself and guard your heart, because the sad reality is that many men are slick, and they will say whatever they feel needs to be said to get what they want. Many men will plant seeds in your mind just like the snake did to Eve in order to get what they want. I can tell you first hand as a man, that once I learned how a woman thinks, it became easy to get what I wanted from them. I knew how to connect with them on an emotional level and manipulate them into give me what I wanted. I watched my guy friends and myself manipulate women over and over again just to have sex with them or have company. So many times, I would be around girls who thought one of my friends loved them, that they were going to one day get married, or one day leave their wife for them, and it never happened. It was all a game. Getting lost in relationship with Jesus will protect you from the game ladies.

Many young women compromise their feelings or what they believe in order to keep a man or make a man who professes to love them happy. You don't have to compromise who you are to keep a man. If it is the right man, you won't have to do those things in order to keep him. He will want you because you are the one God has for him. A man who wants to be kept will be kept and that is just the bottom line sisters.

Some ladies don't see their value in their body, so they throw it around with no regard for the damage that is being done. Other women see the value of it in a negative way, and they use their bodies and charm as a form of manipulation to get the things they want out of life or from a man. They do this out of fear, insecurity, and even pride. Maybe they have made their body an idol and they love for men to praise it and chase after it. The desire of men validates them, and often helps with their insecurity. It really isn't a desire for sex always, but a desire to be connected, accepted, and to feel love. Or, they feel that using their body is a shortcut to getting what they want.

Some women feel that sex is the only thing keeping that man interested in them. Either way, whether they are doing it by choice or because they feel fear, they are still being used. This is very unfortunate. They never realize how special they are in God's eyes and that in reality, they are selling themselves short. God has always had several special purposes for woman since creation and His purpose is not for you to be used. Your body isn't for sport, or to be used just by anybody. When a man and woman come together, they become one, but we will talk about that later. Be careful ladies if you struggle with manipulating men. This is a form of witchcraft and some even call it the Jezebel spirit. If you find yourself using your body, lies, and your influence to get what you what, and get where you want God is not pleased with that. If you walk in manipulation, this shows that you really don't trust God to work out things for your life.

In the previous chapter, we see that God gave Adam a job before He gave Him a wife. Now, I don't know if Adam was getting distracted or got discouraged walking around in paradise, but something caused God to say in the middle of that perfect garden that it was not good for man to be alone. That statement right there speaks volumes about how special a woman is. Paradise wasn't good enough and it needed a woman's touch!

> The Lord God said, "It is not good for the man to
> be alone. I will make a helper suitable for him."
> (Gen. 2:18, NIV)

From the very dawn of time, God looked at man and said, "Uh-oh, man needs some help!" God gave Adam a task to complete and the authority to do it, but God realized that wasn't enough. The story says that God caused a deep sleep to fall on Adam, and He removed a rib from Adam's side and formed Eve. Right there, we see two more profound facts about women. God created Eve from Adam's side. He never desired for the woman to be thought of as less than, but more as a partner. He didn't pull Eve from Adam's back or feet, so she is not behind him, or below him. She is at her husband's side joined as one flesh in God's eyes. You also notice that the ribs protect the lungs. Our lungs help us breath in the oxygen that gives us life.

A man can breathe in many things in this life. God will breathe a vision, a dream, and an anointing on his life, and the woman as the rib must help protect what God has placed inside of that man's spiritual lungs. The enemy will always try to come and puncture the spiritual lung to drain the life out of your man's dream, vision, or strength in God. I often say that God made man the head, but women are the neck. A woman has the power to influence her man to look to the left or to the right, and make him aware of things he may not see. A smart man will always consider the counsel of a woman who is really for him and loves him. A smart man knows how to appreciate the rib that God gave him.

Sadly, this is where many women and men go wrong. They take what God put inside of them and try to fulfill a legitimate desire in an illegitimate place. God created women to be a helpmate, and that is often why many women get caught up with a bad guy. They waste time and effort investing in a man who is not doing right by them or not amounting to much. They take the desire God created in them to be a helpmate and use it to help the wrong guy. Have you wasted your time, body, or resources trying to help the wrong men? You may wonder how you know if you are jumping into a relationship that will be a waste of your time.

I mentioned above that many women try to use their body, sweet words, or manipulation to catch a man. This is the first warning sign that you are headed into a disaster. The Bible never tells a woman to try to catch, seduce, or chase after a man. If you are doing any of these things, it is not from God. The Bible says clearly, "He who finds a wife finds a good thing, And obtains favor from the Lord" (Prov. 18:22, NKJV).

Ladies, a man is supposed to find you! You don't have to flag him down and say, "Hey, I am right here, look at me! I am the one for you. Appreciate me! Love me! Marry me! Don't date her, she is not the one for you, I am!" You do not have to put yourselves out there for everyone to see. When you put it all out there for everyone to see, you will attract more wolves than you do good men. The cheapest prices always attract the most customers. When you put yourself on the clearance rack, you make any man think he can have access to you when, in reality, he can't afford you. See, most men who see women putting themselves out there, or being desperate for attention, know how to play a woman like that easily. They know she obviously wants attention, so they have a this for that mindset. I will give her what she wants and manipulate her into giving me what I want. Often times, men will get what they want and leave or continue to drink from that well as long as there is a bucket hanging saying drink from me.

Ladies, stop putting the bucket out there for men to grab. Your water should be so deep and hidden in God that any man who walks past your well will keep it moving if they don't have the proper equipment to get to your water. The right man of God is going to walk up to your well with a bucket and plenty of rope in hand. He will see you are worth the effort it takes to set everything up to be able to have the God-given right through marriage to draw from you and drink. I said once before that it is kind of like a man going to a car dealership to buy a car. Now, please don't get offended, but just try to understand the picture that I am painting. Many guys look at women, and they are window shoppers. They have no intentions on taking the car home and actually purchasing it and making a commitment to making it theirs. They just want to go to the parking lot, take it for a ride, and drop it back off at the dealership.

The problem is when ladies allow this to happen, they are putting miles on themselves. Over time, this has effects. You may have let a guy sit in the car take it for a ride and spill a mess all over the seats, and he shouldn't have ever been able to even sit in it. Many ladies give themselves to guys who couldn't handle them, lead them, or be what they needed in a man. Pretty much like saying he couldn't even afford to buy the car he just took for a test drive. Ladies, don't leave that parking lot until God has sent the right guy to take you off of it.

Women who put all this effort into trying to catch a man do not know their worth. You must understand that you are God's daughter, and God loves you more than you could ever imagine. You are special and you are the apple of God's eye. It is not His desire for His daughter to be in a bad relationship where she is being abused, cheated on, and taken for granted. Many women find themselves in these situations because they left the protection of their heavenly Father. Some women do it because they are following their carnal desires. Others may have gone through some terrible things as a child or young woman and are trying to find a way to fill a void or heal a wound. Either way you look at it, God still loves you and wants to take care of you. Ladies, all you need to do is keep the well pure, don't poison the waters. It is not your job to show a man how to be a man. It is not your job to show him how to rig the rope and bucket and be a provider, be a protector, be an encourager, and be a man of God. Your well is your body, your mind, your resources, your talents, your time, and anything else you have to offer.

The way you protect yourselves from getting into a relationship with the wrong man is by hiding yourself in Jesus. Lose yourself in your relationship with God. Don't worry about finding a man or being lonely. Take your time being single to allow God to show you who you are as a woman. Just like we mentioned in the previous chapter with the man, the same pattern must be followed for woman. If you don't know who you are as a woman, you will often look for a man to define that for you. There are many women who get involved with men and change their whole lifestyle, convictions, and desires to follow his. They lose themselves becoming a helpmate to someone they don't fit in with. They end up compromising who they are in order to not be rejected, break up a family, or fear of not being able to provide for themselves or their children. This is often described as a toxic relationship. The reason the relationship is toxic is because you are in an environment that was not designed for you to thrive, grow, excel, and be everything God has created you to be. You have placed yourself in a place that is destroying you, hurting you, killing your self-esteem, and allowing the enemy to steal your identity in Jesus Christ!

You are a rib, but you can't just be any man's rib. It don't matter how sweet you are, how pretty you look, how hard you try, if it is not where God created you to fit in, you will never fit in. You keep trying to fit in, and make it work, but he keeps rejecting you because you are not his. He keeps letting you down emotionally, cheating on you, doing you wrong, making you have to provide and be the man in the relationship because you have tried to fit in somewhere you don't belong! The problem is that many women marry or have children by men whom God never intended for them. After spending years of trying to figure it out, they often find themselves in a dark hole of depression. When they finally get the courage to try to climb out, they have kids, heartache, old age, and so much baggage. It was quick falling into the bad situation, having kids, and getting in debt, but it is harder and may take longer to climb out and heal. Bitterness tries to kick in because you are carrying weight that God never designed you for.

This all starts with knowing your worth, and having faith that Jesus loves you ladies. If you get lost in Jesus, the only way a man will be able to find you is if he has directions from God. If your heart is in God's hands, a man will not be able to access it, unless He went through God first. When a man is praying, seeking God, and is ready to be blessed with a wife, God will give him the spiritual GPS to the woman's location that is designed for him.

Am I saying that a woman's life should revolve around waiting for a man to come sweep her off of her feet so she can live in her purpose? No, not at all. What I am saying is that ladies must have their focus on the right things. Focus on your relationship with

God, your talents, your likes, your education, and get busy being a woman of God. By the time a man comes into your life, all he should do is compliment the process God has already started in your life. Too many women are looking for a man to complete them, but no man will ever be able to do that. Too many women are looking for a man to fix their broken hearts from past relationships or heal father wounds from having an absentee father, but no man can do that. Many women are looking for a man to be things that only God can be and do things that only God can do. I am not saying men are useless, but I am saying many times what a woman is expecting of a man, she already has in God. If she would turn to God for those things, she wouldn't open herself up to any man that comes along and fails to meet their expectations or fulfill their desires.

Don't look for a man to be God; wait for a man that compliments what God is already doing in your life. God is the one who can heal you, love you, and show you your purpose in life. Any man of God that comes into your life will only assist God in doing the things God has already started in your life. When you focus on being the best woman you can be for God and a man of God is doing the same thing, you become a powerful team for the kingdom when God brings you together, and that is what it is all about.

What the enemy loves to do with women is poison their waters by destroying their self-worth. He knows that if he can poison her, he can poison her husband who comes to drink from her, and he can poison her children who she feeds and nurtures. By damaging one woman, he can cause damage to generations! That is why he loves to get a woman to look in the mirror or at her past and be devastated. He knows that depression opens the doors to bitterness, and bitterness opens the doors to compromise and sin.

Many women struggle with molestation or father wounds. The enemy loves to play on these things and make them feel less than what they really are. He does not want them to value their bodies and know their worth in God's eyes. Many women often find themselves in a relationship that they know is not good for them, but they feel it is the best they can do because their self-image has been destroyed. There are other woman who simply struggle with lust, being bored, or fear of being alone, and they can only overcome this through the power and direction of Jesus Christ.

From the dawn of time, God created woman to be nurtures and helpers. When a woman gives her body to a man, it feeds a God-given hunger and desire that is in him and through this act can produce life. When a woman is pregnant, the baby feeds off of whatever the mother eats. When the baby is born, it feeds off the milk produced by the mother's body. A woman has a very hard job. Her family is constantly depending and feeding off of her in numerous ways.

The enemy would love to poison the well of the woman, so in turn he can poison everyone else feeding off of that woman. Ladies, you have the power to affect generations. Eve, through her actions and influence, affected all of mankind. How will you use the power you have in this world? You can be nurturing the next president, revival preacher, prophet, teacher, and so much more. That is a great power and responsibility. The society we live in will try to downplay this and make woman feel they need to be more like men. They will make you feel like what you are doing is not important, but the fact is that without women, nothing would happen. Behind every great man or woman, there is a woman who gave them life, nurtured them, raised them, loved them, or stood by their side during a hard time. No person will ever come though this life without the influence of a woman on them, whether good or bad.

Ladies, it is time to take the bucket down. You don't need to advertise or make your water available to anyone. You can't let just anyone drink from your well. You may have a good heart and good intentions, but the waters of your energy, your time, your body, and your resources are not for everybody. Focus on your relationship with God, and the rest will fall into place. Your job, your ministry, your desires, your family, your husband, and everything else will fall into place when you lose yourself in Jesus. The Bible describes what a Godly woman is, and this is what all woman of God should aspire to be. Focus on being these things, and never let the enemy make you feel like you are not important. You are special to God, you are a valuable jewel on this earth. Don't waste the jewel by putting it in a fools hands who does not know how to use it and invest it wisely.

Who can find a virtuous woman? for her price is far above rubies.

The heart of her husband doth safely trust in her, so that he shall have no need of spoil.

She will do him good and not evil all the days of her life.

She seeketh wool, and flax, and worketh willingly with her hands.

She is like the merchants' ships; she bringeth her food from afar.

She riseth also while it is yet night, and giveth meat to her household, and a portion to her maidens.

She considereth a field, and buyeth it: with the fruit of her hands she planteth a vineyard.

She girdeth her loins with strength, and strengtheneth her arms.

She perceiveth that her merchandise is good: her candle goeth not out by night.

She layeth her hands to the spindle, and her hands hold the distaff.

She stretcheth out her hand to the poor; yea, she reacheth forth her hands to the needy.

She is not afraid of the snow for her household: for all her household are clothed with scarlet.

She maketh herself coverings of tapestry; her clothing is silk and purple.

Her husband is known in the gates, when he sitteth among the elders of the land.

She maketh fine linen, and selleth it; and delivereth girdles unto the merchant.

Strength and honour are her clothing; and she shall rejoice in time to come.

She openeth her mouth with wisdom; and in her tongue is the law of kindness.

She looketh well to the ways of her household, and eateth not the bread of idleness.

Her children arise up, and call her blessed; her husband also, and he praiseth her.

Many daughters have done virtuously, but thou excellest them all.

Favour is deceitful, and beauty is vain: but a woman that feareth the Lord, she shall be praised.

Give her of the fruit of her hands; and let her own works praise her in the gates. (Prov. 31:10–31)

CHAPTER 4

From You and I to Us

Wherefore they are no more twain, but one flesh.
What therefore God hath joined together,
let not man put asunder.
— Matthew 19:6, KJV

There are things that God expects from you as an individual, and there are things that God expects from you as a unit when you become married. A Godly marriage will follow biblical principles. You may have read the previous chapters and said, "I did all of that. I am doing what God expects from me as a man or woman." But, with a new title comes a new role. When you make the transition into becoming a husband or wife, there are certain added responsibilities, requirements, and guidelines that God and your spouse will put into place. If you follow these things, your marriage will be blessed. The problem people run into when they get married is they find out that following these guidelines and meeting these responsibilities often requires us to die to self. You find out fast that any successful marriage is familiar with sacrifice. If you are selfish and not willing to compromise or sacrifice, your marriage will be miserable. We live in a generation of people looking at relationship goals on the internet and saying they want that, but they don't want the work that it took to get to the goal. People want the blessing without the sacrifice, and the crown without the cross.

No matter how much chemistry, how much sex, how much fun, or how much money you have, two people will not always see eye to eye. Your personalities and how you respond to certain situations will cause disagreements occasionally. Two people will not always wake up and be riding the same wave of happiness or energy. You will both individually have your share of good days, bad days, and disagreements. There will even be some days when both of you are going through a hard time and you both feel completely drained. What happens when you both look to each other to be the strong one, but you both are too tired to hold each other up? What happens when your spouse asks you to do something that you really don't want to do, but they are very excited about it? What happens when mean words are exchanged, and both of you feel like the other one is in the wrong and should apologize first? What happens when the unexpected happens and catches the family by surprise? What happens when you don't agree with how you deal with children, money, or problems that may arise? Even though you become one, you will still have your individual feelings about things. I have seen people say that they will know everything they need to know from the first kiss, and this is one of the most ridiculous things I have ever heard. Chemistry can be built and learned. Some of you done kissed somebody and walked away from the love of your life thinking you didn't have chemistry. It takes patience, being humble, and being willing to sacrifice, but chemistry can be built in a marriage.

In marriage, sometimes, you will have to put your feelings to the side to benefit your spouse, the marriage, or simply just because your feelings about something are not right. Our flesh does not like this. This is why God has set guidelines in His word for how individuals, and later husbands and wives, should carry themselves. God has an order for life and if we follow this order, we will be victorious! Your pride may take a hit in order for there to be peace in your marriage and home.

From the beginning of time, God set order to things. He separated the day from the night, and He placed the earth close enough to the sun that we don't freeze, but far away enough that we don't burn up. He set the seasons into motion, and created everything in time and space. Everything God created has a purpose, function, and role to play. When God created something and He was finished, He said it was good. What this says about God is He has all the measurements. Just like a tailored suit requires measurement, God has all of the numbers down. He knows just how many miles the earth needed to be away from the sun, and I am sure He knows what is best for you. If God can keep the universe in order, the oceans in place, and set the stars and moon in the sky, He can bring an order into our life that will work for us the way the galaxies work for Him. The way that God created everything to be and the order He put things in were good. If we follow this order, we will live a blessed, victorious, and fulfilling life.

The problem is many times what God wants and what we feel we want don't add up. Many times, instead of trusting God and the principles found in His word, we prefer to take matters into our own hands and fight dirty in order to have our way. For now, let's talk about what God expects from husbands and wives, and later on, we will discuss fighting dirty in marriage and the damage it causes.

I have seen wives who envy the role or power they feel that God has given the husband, and I have seen husbands who feel that wives have it easy. I will tell you right now neither role is easy, nor are both roles impossible without the guidance of the Holy Spirit. If you could switch places with your spouse, you would see that it is not easier being them. I often tell my soldiers in the army that it is always easy to complain about your sergeant and how he operates, but you don't know what it takes to be a sergeant. You don't know what it takes to walk in his boots and, if you did, you might find out quickly that you wouldn't even survive.

People always look at situations and say what they would have done if it was them or if they were in that position, but the reality is that they don't have a clue what they would do until they actually get in that position. Looking at the position from the outside perspective is completely different than actually sitting in the position and carrying the weight, the attacks, and the pressure of choices that must be made that come with that seat.

> For the husband is the head of the wife, even as
> Christ is the head of the church: and he is the

savior of the body. Husbands, love your wives, even as Christ also loved the church, and gave himself for it; That he might sanctify and cleanse it with the washing of water by the word, That he might present it to himself a glorious church, not having spot, or wrinkle, or any such thing; but that it should be holy and without blemish. So ought men to love their wives as their own bodies. He that loveth his wife loveth himself. For no man ever yet hated his own flesh; but nourisheth and cherisheth it, even as the Lord the church: For we are members of his body, of his flesh, and of his bones. For this cause shall a man leave his father and mother, and shall be joined unto his wife, and they two shall be one flesh. This is a great mystery: but I speak concerning Christ and the church. Nevertheless let every one of you in particular so love his wife even as himself. (Eph. 5:23–33)

In the world we live in today, many women and feminist groups would get turned off by that very first statement. The Bible says the husband is the head of the wife. Many men may have read this and felt their chest puff up, but this is no easy task, nor does it mean that your wife is your slave, or beneath you. Two verses down it says to love your wives as Christ loved the church and gave Himself for it. You must look at the significance of what Jesus went through during His crucifixion for you and me. If we stopped right here, and this was the only requirement for husbands, it would still be almost impossible. God is calling for husband to love their wives as Christ loved the church. Everybody who goes to church is not easy to love. Everybody who goes to church is not living right. There are people who cheat, lie, steal, and are the most evil people sitting right in the front row. The Pharisees in the Bible were always at the synagogue teaching the people and John the Baptist called them vipers. But when Jesus hung on the cross, His love did not discriminate.

He did not say I am laying down my life for the righteous, the good looking, the kind hearted, the goodie two shoes, the perfect, or only those who love me back! He gave his life because of His great love for you and me. There is nothing we can do to deserve that love. There is no sin we could do that would make Him stop loving us. There is literally nothing that can conquer the act of love He displayed on that cross. God died for the best and the worse of people, and He loved them equally. He didn't hang on the cross longer for the people who didn't like Him, and He didn't take less of a beating for the ones who did. There was one price and one act of love that was enough for everybody.

What does this mean for a husband? It means you must make sure God is the one who led you to the woman you are thinking about marrying. If you are to follow this scripture, it means no matter what your wife does you must love her. God didn't strike you down every time you did wrong, He loved you so much He forgave you time and time again for your sins, and showed great patience with you. Your love is a representation of Christ in you. Through your actions with your wife, Christ should be reflected in everything you do. She could be the worse wife in the world, but you must love her, and not only that lay down your life for her.

Many people take that as literally, but it is much more than that. You can lay down your life in other ways. Maybe your wife is not the easiest woman to love. Maybe you start thinking that some other woman would treat you better. It actually may be possible that some other woman out there treated you better or would treat you better, but you must lay down your desires to do what you want, or follow what you feel, and give your life up in sacrifice. You may have to get up early in the morning and pray, and fast for your wife and family like never before. You may have to show her love and receive none in return. Just like Jesus died for you and me when we were in sin, you must do the same. Jesus died for everyone who has ever existed, and some of them never returned that love back.

You think it was easy for Jesus to love us? He prayed in the garden the night before for the cup to pass from Him. He struggled when He carried that cross. I am sure He screamed in pain when they beat Him and put nails in His hands and feet. I know it was a humbling feeling being dragged through the street, spit on, and hung naked for the world to see, but He endured it all because of His amazing love. He has called you to love your wife in that same manner. He has called you to take up your cross and follow Him. He has called for the husband to truly be Christ-like. This is why you need to take your vows and covenant you make between you, a woman, and God seriously. You are not only promising these things to a woman, but you are making a promise before God. That is why you need to acknowledge God when you choose a wife. The Bible says:

> But at the beginning of creation God 'made them male and female. For this reason a man will leave his father and mother and be united to his wife, and the two will become one flesh. So they are no longer two, but one flesh. Therefore what God has joined together, let no one separate. (Mark 10:6–9)

The Bible then goes on to call husbands to love their wives as they love themselves. You love yourself so you are going to take care of yourself. If you are hungry, you will eat. If you feel like treating yourself, you will. You are going to take care of your needs the best way you can. God requires a husband to love his wife in that same way. What does that mean? It means you must look at your wives needs as if they were your very own. If you want an ice cream in the middle of the night, you will go get it if you want it badly enough. If you are lying in bed and you are nice and comfortable and your wife ask you for an ice cream from the fridge in the middle of the night, you should respect her need as if it were your own. This may seem a little extreme and funny, but you must do for your wife what you would do for yourself.

The beauty of this is that even though the Bible calls the husband the head, it also requires him to have an attitude of servanthood to his wife. So, all of you men who got puffed up when you read that you are the head, allow this point to deflate your ego. God gave you great position and responsibility, but He also gave you a wife in order to keep you humble. God can't work with pride, so He put somethings into place to help you keep that in check. Now, of course, many women are reading this and grinning from ear to ear, but this does not mean you can abuse this. We will get to that in a moment.

What we can conclude from what we read earlier about Adam, and what we read later in the New Testament, is that man is the head of the woman. God requires man to work, to provide, to protect, to guide, and to love His wife as He loved the church. It is impossible to do these things even with the best of wives without being constantly on your face before God. God will hold you accountable for where you lead your family. It is your responsibility to seek God for direction and carry out what He instructs you. You may have to get up when your family is still sleeping in order to seek God's face. You will need to have balance, patience, and all the fruits of the Spirit in order to carry all of this out. You cannot get so caught up in a ministry you neglect your family, or get so caught up in providing you are never around to lead your family. You will have to lean on God for strength and direction to be the kind of man that God has called you to be. If you choose wisely, God will give you a helpmate instead of a deadweight.

If you look at the story of Adam and Eve, God gave Adam authority and dominion, and because of His failure to step into His God-given role, his family suffered and got removed from paradise. God had given Adam authority over his wife and the animals in the garden. If you read the story of Adam and Eve, the Bible never says that Eve went to find Adam when she was talking to the snake. It says she turned and gave Adam the fruit to eat. Adam failed to step up and be the man for his family. He was there the entire time Eve was talking to the snake. He let Eve run the show, and the result was disaster. Adam should have taken the dominion and authority God had given him and rebuked that snake, grabbed his wife by the hand, and said, "We will not eat from this tree." He should have had the mindset of Joshua! Check out this awesome verse.

> But if serving the LORD seems undesirable to
> you, then choose for yourselves this day whom
> you will serve, whether the gods your ancestors
> served beyond the Euphrates, or the gods of the
> Amorites, in whose land you are living. But as for
> me and my household, we will serve the LORD.
> (Josh. 24:15, NIV)

You must be very aware of the enemy's attacks against your family. You must constantly stand on guard, watching, praying, and fasting. The enemy will try to discourage you, tempt you with lust, overload you, or cripple you with bitterness. We often see many men who don't speak out on what they are going through, or feeling. Many guys are taught it is not masculine to speak about how you feel. You keep all of that stuff bottled inside and buried deep. Many guys never speak up and end up going into auto pilot or being bullied around by their wives. This causes there to be a void that the enemy tries to fill with bitterness. If the enemy can get you to be bitter toward your wife, he will try to tempt you with lust.

Many men live in the silence of shadows. They get tired of arguing with their wives or hoping things will change. They get tired of praying and have too much pride to go to counseling, or maybe think it won't help. Some guys feel that if they said how they really feel, their wives would not be able to handle it and there would be serious repercussions. Because of this, many men sneak around in the shadows of silence. They are silent in their pain, and they are silent when they cheat. Instead of having the faith that God can change their wives, their situation, or to try things like counseling, they give into the bitterness. Men, you cannot let the enemy steal your joy and make you bitter. The Bible says the joy of the Lord is your strength.

You must keep the faith no matter what is going on with your emotions, your job, or your family. You must always remind yourself that spiritual warfare is real and you are the head of your family. You are a line of defense and the enemy wants to break those walls down. You must stand on your watch tower and fight off the enemy. He may use your family, your wife, or your job against you, but understand it is not personal. Don't be angry with your wife. The Bible says in 1 Peter 3:7, "Husbands, in the same way be considerate as you live with your wives, and treat them with respect as the weaker partner and as heirs with you of the gracious gift of life, so that nothing will hinder your prayers." Another verse every man should keep hidden in their heart is this one stated in Ephesians 6:12, "For our struggle is not against flesh and blood, but against the rulers, against the authorities, against the powers of this dark world and against the spiritual forces of evil in the heavenly realms."

You must treat your wives as the weaker partner. This does not excuse them for bad behavior, but you need to know that the attack is not personal. Your fight isn't against your wife, but against the powers of darkness. The enemy is not after your marriage. He is after your faith and your territory. The Bible says to give no place to the devil. You can't let the enemy get a foot in your house, and if he does you need to learn how to exercise your dominion, power, and authority and rebuke him. You must learn who the enemy is and how to fight the right way. Many times, couples fight dirty and cause more damage than good. We will talk about this in a later chapter.

Men, understand that the enemy would love more than anything to take the head off the body. If you remove the head from the body, the body has no vision. Have you ever heard of the phrase, "A chicken running around with no head?" There are so many broken families because either a man started a family with the wrong woman, or he failed to follow biblical principle in how he dealt with his wife. You have single mothers running around trying to do the job of a man and be a daddy, and no matter how good they are, they cannot be you.

This is why so many children are hurting and grow up repeating the same mistakes their parents made. Just like Adam watched Eve eat from the tree and did nothing, men stand back and watch a home collapse and single mothers trying to do it on their own. You are called to be the head and covering for your family. You must understand that this is going to come with great spiritual warfare. If the enemy can take you out of the picture, he has much easier access to your wife and children. He could do damage to generations just because of your failure to step up and be the man God has called you to be. It sounds good to be the head, but understand being the head comes with great attack, and heavy burdens. Being the head makes you a giant target.

I want you to notice that there are no stipulations to what God has instructed for husbands. You cannot have conditional love. Your love cannot be quid pro quo. Regardless of how your wife is behaving, you must love her through it all. The same goes for women when we talk about what God has asked of them. There are no conditions saying, "What if this? What if that? You don't have to do this if they are doing this." Many people struggle with this because they feel they are losing out, or it is an unfair deal. This is where your faith must kick in, and you realize that everything you do, you do it unto the Lord. If God ask you to do something, but you don't feel like the person deserves what God has asked you to do, you do it anyway. This is a key to living a blessed life. You are not doing what God ask because people deserve it, you are doing it because you love God, and you trust Him with your life.

We have talked about husbands, and what God has required of them, so let us move on to the wives. As we read above, it is not an easy job being a husband. The husband has a lot on his plate, but this does not mean that the wives job is any less difficult or important.

> An excellent wife is the crown of her husband,
> but she who brings shame is like rottenness in his
> bones. (Prov. 12:4, ESV)

What kind of wife are you going to be? Are you going to be a biblical wife or a worldly one? We live in a world of social media memes that brag or make fun of being a difficult wife. We live in a world where a man is considered weak if he cannot handle a strong woman. Strong woman is sometimes code for difficult to deal with. Often times, what they mean by strong woman is a woman who is loud, voices her opinion regardless of the consequences, lacks self-control or humility, has many unhealed wounds, and does not respect the order God has set in place.

I often wonder why women feel the need to be handled. A zoo animal is something that needs to be handled, a wife is not. God never calls for a woman to be under or less than a man, but there are certain qualities laid out in scripture for her to implement into her life. The world will tell women to be loud, bold, and have a fighter attitude, but this is not what God calls for at all. God calls for woman in several verses to have a gentle spirit about them. Many women will tell you this is weakness and oppressive thinking, but it actually takes much strength and great faith in God to actually carry yourself in this manner.

> Likewise, wives, be subject to your own husbands, so that even if some do not obey the word, they may be won without a word by the conduct of their wives, when they see your respectful and pure conduct. Do not let your adorning be external—the braiding of hair and the putting on of gold jewelry, or the clothing you wear— but let your adorning be the hidden person of the heart with the imperishable beauty of a gentle and quiet spirit, which in God's sight is very precious. For this is how the holy women who hoped in God used to adorn themselves, by submitting to their own husbands. (1 Pet. 3:1–6, ESV)

> Wives, submit yourselves unto your own husbands, as unto the Lord. Nevertheless let every one of you in particular so love his wife even as himself; and the wife see that she reverence her husband. (Eph. 5:22, 33)

These verses call for wives to reverence, respect, and not bring shame unto her husband. In the verse down below, it says an excellent wife has her husband's trust, and she does him good and not harm all the days of her life. The reason I bring this up is because society has taken on the spirit of the antichrist. This means anything

God has set in order, the enemy tries to destroy it. If the Bible calls for man and woman to act a certain way and play a certain role, the enemy will try to defy that and influence people to live contrary to how the Bible calls us to live.

Many women believe a man is supposed to take whatever she throws at him, and if he can't handle it, he is not a real man. Now, the Bible does call for husbands to love their wives unconditionally, but it works hand in hand with what God asks of a wife. If both husband and wife are doing what God has asked, no one will feel like they are being taken advantage of or being treated unfairly. I often say it is a man's job to respect a woman and it is a woman's job to give him something to respect. This goes back to individual responsibility to God. We mentioned in previous chapters what it means to be a Godly man or woman of God. If both of you are already living out these things before you are married, it will be so much easier to do what God is asking you to do in scriptures as a married couple.

Society has brainwashed women into thinking it is okay to let emotions run wild. This is part of being a woman, and men just need to deal with it. Excuses for some extreme behaviors range from hormones to periods and pregnancy. The problem with this is as a child of God, the Spirit of God living inside of you should be stronger than all these. Plus, we could argue that these excuses are complete hypocrisy. If you go to work, you don't disrespect your boss or let your emotions fly off the handle. You keep it in check because you want to get your check and not get fired. The Holy Spirit should help you keep it in check because you want to be pleasing in God's eyes. Do you value money more than you value God looking down at you with pleasure? You respect and submit to your boss, and you must do the same unto your husband. The Bible says to submit yourselves as unto the Lord. However, your respect to your husband should be a reflection of how you respect God. Just like I mentioned with what God has asked the man to do, this may seem almost impossible at times. How can you submit to an imperfect man the same way you submit to a perfect God?

I am going to talk about something that affects many women in marriage. The enemy's plan is always to break up a home, and one of the ways he does this is by always enticing the woman to become a runner. This is why the Bible calls for wives not to leave their husbands. The Bible says for us not to be ignorant of Satan's devices. I mentioned that men must get up and cover the family in prayer. I believe also that women can control the spiritual climate of the house. Ladies, you have power in your home! You need to set the tone for your house through worship, praise, prayer, and seeking God. People often joke and say happy wife, happy life. Yes, your husband and your children can make you happy, but that is not their responsibility and they cannot make you happy like Jesus can. So, your happiness is really your responsibility because it is your choice how much you expose yourself to the presence of God. The more you expose yourself to the presence of God, the more your eyes will open, and your faith will increase. The enemy has tried so hard to belittle, and destroy the wife's role and the importance she plays. I want to show you what the Bible says about a good wife.

> An excellent wife who can find? She is far more
> precious than jewels. The heart of her husband
> trusts in her, and he will have no lack of gain. She
> does him good, and not harm, all the days of her
> life. (Prov. 31:10–31, ESV)

The Bible says an excellent wife is precious. It goes on to describe some of the characteristics of what makes her excellent. It says the heart of her husband trusts her. Can your husband trust you? Have you built a foundation of trust or lies in your marriage? Many women struggle with lying because of shame. They may have been hurt, or used in the past, and they bury it down deep. The problem is these old wounds always take an effect on the marriage. With many couples I have talked to, unaddressed wounds from the past always pop up later in the marriage.

Instead of waiting for the earthquake and dealing with the aftermath, it is best to be upfront and honest at the start of the marriage and seek counseling. Many women use lies and manipulation to paint a picture or get what they want, but this is not the way of a Godly wife. The verse also goes on to say that she does her husband good and not harm all the days of her life. Do you build your husband up, or do you tear him down? Do you support his dream and respect his role as head of the family, or do you always undermine, belittle him, and make him feel less than a man? One thing I have noticed is society makes so many excuses for bad behavior. They have a justification for everything, but in God's eyes there is none. You have to be honest with yourself. I have learned that when people don't want to do right, they will always find an excuse to justify them not doing right. So, if you don't want to submit, you will always find a reason not to.

You have power and influence with your husband, even though the enemy would have you thinking otherwise. What you do affects him, and how he sees himself. They say when a man doesn't trust his wife, he is just insecure, but women never ask the question, "Is there something I have done or a lie I have told to make my husband feel like he can't trust me?" A wise woman can look in the mirror and take responsibility for her actions, and use the power she has in marriage to build her husband, her family, and her home up as opposed to tearing it down.

Many women in this day and age don't want to take responsibility for anything. That is why there are so many broken homes. There are many men who treat women badly, and they deserve to be divorced and on child support, but there are many women who are lazy and use the system to their advantage. I have seen many women who want to have the benefits of being a wife without the responsibility of actually being one. Many women take their kids and become runners. Instead of praying, fasting, and taking control of the atmosphere in their home, they quit. Pride tells many women they could do a better job than their husbands, so they take the child support or alimony, and put their faith in that and their own abilities and quit on the marriage. But, like we mentioned before, there were vows made before God that need to be taken seriously. You promised for richer or poor, better or worse, and God does not take that lightly. Many times, women can be under the influence of the spirit of the Antichrist and not even realize it. The spirit of the antichrist will always try to come against and destroy God's order for things.

So, since God has created man as the head of the family, the spirit of the anti Christ will always influence you to go against that standard the Lord has set.

I want to be clear that the Bible says divorce is an option if adultery is committed, and I am a firm believer that no woman should stay in an abusive relationship, but I do believe God needs to be acknowledged and counseling should take place before any final decisions are made. I have seen many women uproot their children and leave just because they didn't like the situation. They justified the behavior by exaggerating abuse. For instance, if someone tells you something you don't like about yourself, that is not verbal abuse. If I say, "Hey, you are a liar," that does not mean I am verbally abusing you. Like I said in a previous paragraph, people will always find an excuse and justification to do what they want to do.

Just make sure you are being honest with yourself and seeking God before any choices are made. You need to be able to tell the difference between the voice of God, the voice of the enemy, and your own voice. The enemy's goal is always to destroy your home, and he will offer as many justifications as he can in order to get you to give up on your marriage, or rebel against your husband.

Many women hear the word, "submit," and they cringe. The problem is that both people need to understand that there is nothing wrong with the system God has put into place. We mess it all up by skipping steps. People jump into marriage and find out the husband is lazy and doesn't mind not having a job, or the wife doesn't know how to let the man be the man.

Now, the Bible is calling for obedience without conditions, but many wives and husbands feel they don't have to, or, they don't want to because their spouse is neither meeting their expectations, nor the expectations of the Bible. Just like husbands should love their wives regardless of her behavior, a wife must respect and honor her husband regardless of his. If you can't do it for him, do it because you love God.

Many people can never be blessed or receive the promises of God because they get stuck here. She doesn't deserve my love, so I am not going to give it. He doesn't deserve my respect, so I am not going to give it. Really what you are saying to God is "because I don't like my conditions, I am not going to obey what you have asked of me." This shows you have no faith. Faith will allow you to obey the word of God, even when your circumstances don't look promising. The Bible says without faith, it is impossible to please God! This is why it is so important to focus on being a Godly man or woman of God first before trying to be a Godly husband or wife.

Both the husband and wife need to understand that a bad marriage does not exempt you from doing what God has asked of you. People jump into marriage and skip all of the steps God has put into place and think a miracle is just going to take place. I have alarming news for you! If you were dysfunctional single, you will be dysfunctional married. Don't have unrealistic expectations of your spouse. If you do, you will always be disappointed. What we mentioned in this chapter is what God expects from a husband and a wife. You should expect what God expects from them because we are not greater than God. If you base your marriage off of these principles, everything else will fall into place. In the next chapter, I would like to talk to you about the damage of unrealistic expectations.

CHAPTER 5

Your Spouse Can't Handle Your Expectations

It is better to take refuge in the LORD
than to trust in people.

—Psalm 118:8

D o you find yourself disappointed in your marriage? Do you often find yourself daydreaming about one of your exes, or scrolling through social media fantasizing about being with someone else? Do you feel like your marriage isn't what you thought it would be? Do you feel a lack of motivation and passion? Do you find your happiness dependent on what your spouse is or is not doing? Do you ever finding yourself thinking I wish my spouse was like this or that, but have never really communicated with them? Do you have expectations or desires that you have not communicated with your spouse?

Are your expectations completely selfish and all about your desires, your feelings, and needs being taking care of? Are you loyal to your spouse not just with your body, but with your mind, heart, and conversations? Do you have a work wife or husband whom, though you are not sexually intimate, you are intimate in every other kind of way? Do you find yourself longing for your past, or feeling like you made a big mistake being married to the person you are married to? This is usually do to past disappointment, an improper perspective, lack of communication, and unrealistic expectations. People think the grass will be greener somewhere else, but the reality is sometimes we are just too lazy, too hurt, or too proud to water the grass where we are.

Many times, we entertain bad behavior or thinking patterns because we have the wrong perspective. The enemy has been doing what he does for a very long time and he is good at it. He feeds people with lies and deceptions and causes people to have a false perspective on reality. When this happens, we tend to leave doors open that should be closed. The enemy sneaks in through these doors and causes our eyes, hearts, and sometimes bodies to wonder. If you don't close the door on a small thought, it becomes temptation, and grows into actual action.

Make no mistake about it, entertaining these thoughts is cheating. Going out and actually having sex is not the only way people cheat. The Bible says if you even look at a person to lust after them in your mind, it is the same as already committing the act in God's eyes. Just because you are not doing it with your body, does not mean you are not a cheater. You can break your vows in your mind, long before breaking them with your body.

Are you holding on to an ex's phone number, hoarding old pictures, letters, or keeping tabs on them through social media? Do you find yourself fantasizing that your partner was someone else while being intimate? Are you having secret conversations? Do you have a lock on your phone because you know if your spouse were to go through it they may find something on you?

Instead of thinking things would be better with somebody else, ask yourself have you really done everything you can to make your marriage the best? Many people are always so quick to say yes, but if you talk to their spouse, you would get a completely different answer. You think being with a new person will fix everything, and everything will be way better, with no problems.

Your unrealistic expectations have caused you to be disappointed with what you have. The enemy has used this constant disappointment, to open the door to bitterness. Once the enemy has a foot in the door, he will put his arm in, eventually his shoulder, and then his whole body. Before you know it, you will be in a stronghold. When we compromise and leave doors open, we give the enemy legal access to infiltrate our minds. The problem we have here is eliminating that disappointment you feel toward your spouse, so we can close some of these doors before it is too late. There are somethings that you can't fight in the flesh, and you have to fight in the Spirit. Maybe you have done everything you can do to make your marriage work physically, but maybe there are something in the spirit that need to be addressed, and they can only be broken through fasting, prayer, and spiritual warfare. Remember what we said in earlier chapters about walking in dominion and authority? Have you prayed about it as much as you have complained about it? Have you really spent time in your prayer closet going to war on behalf of your marriage and spouse?

Many times, people have valid reasons to be disappointed with their spouse, but other times they simply don't have a mature perspective on marriage. Sometimes, the reason you are so full of bitterness and disappointment is because your expectations for your spouse were far too high. You wanted them to do things for you that only you or God could do. When they failed to do these things, you start wondering if someone else could meet your expectations, without ever stopping to think that the expectations you have cannot be met by a spouse. Also, maybe you had unrealistic expectations of who they were. People fall in love with potential instead of the person, and then later realize that the person wasn't as in love with their potential as you were.

If you are depending on your spouse for your happiness, you are going to be disappointed. If you are depending on your spouse to erase bad memories or pain from your past, you will be disappointed. If you are in a mess in your life, and you are expecting marriage to perform a magic trick and make it all disappear, you will be disappointed. If you are looking for your spouse to have all the answers, never let you down, argue, or disagree with you, you are going to be disappointed. Many times we overreact when our spouse falls short in certain areas. Sometimes, we need to forgive and take it to God in prayer.

Many marriages are miserable because the spouses spend years trying to hammer away at each other. They believe that if they just say that right point at the right time in the argument, their spouse is going to get it together. They believe if they leave for a few weeks or threaten to divorce or cheat, their spouse will wake up and get the picture.

This is called fighting dirty, and we will talk about this in the next chapter. The problem is that people need to realize that all the fighting in the world wouldn't change the fact that some things aren't worth fighting over because your spouse could never meet the expectations you are asking them to meet. Like I mentioned in the previous chapter, it is okay to expect from your spouse what God expects from them, but you need to make sure you are not making your spouse an idol.

I believe sometimes God will allow our spouse not to get it right and keep them in the dark sometimes just to show us to learn to depend, trust, and lean on Him. For instance, you wait around all day for your husband to come home so you can vent about your problems. There is nothing wrong with wanting to talk to your husband about your day, but when he comes home and he is not being a very good listener or acting like he does not care, this will frustrate you. It is reasonable to expect for your husband to listen to your concerns, feelings, and problems, but sometimes, I believe God will allow everyone to let you down just so He can pick you up. God will say, "You waited for him all day, but I was here all along. You complain about all of your problems but you never come to me and cast your cares into my hands."

I believe that God will often allow your situation not to change until you learn to put Him first in your life.

Expecting your spouse to listen to you is a realistic expectation, but expecting them to be the source of your happiness is not. Your spouse, no matter how good they are, will not always be in the mood to listen, and will not always say the right things, remember your requests, or even honor how you feel, but God will. You may have wounds from your past that resurface during marriage. You can't expect your spouse to know what to do with that, how to fix it, or heal you, but God can.

What I am saying in a nutshell is that you can't expect imperfect people to be perfect. If your happiness, peace, sanity, self-worth, and whole life is dependent on what your spouse is, does, and doesn't do, you will be riding an emotional rollercoaster for the rest of your life.

When your spouse is letting you down in a certain area, you have to be wise about how you handle it. Some people belittle and attack the weakness they see in the spouse and cause more damage than good. Some spouses withdraw themselves emotionally and physically and become bitter. Other spouses call family, friends, and get on social media to express how their spouse is letting them down. Many spouses try to fill in the missing pieces in their marriage with someone else of the opposite sex. All of these tactics will result in disaster and only cause more damage than good.

The first thing you need to do is not take all of your partner's failures as a personal attack. Maybe your spouse is not the greatest with money. Maybe they are not the best at communicating how they really feel toward you. Maybe the way they express their love does not match the way you receive or communicate yours. None of these failures mean that your spouse does not love or care about you.

Often times, you need to look at the root of the problem. People who have bad spending habits usually have some deeper issue going on. They may be trying to impress you through spending money for several different reasons. Maybe they believe, because of past experiences, if they don't throw the money around, you won't stay with them. Maybe they grew up, and they never had anything, and when they got a job, they just couldn't stop spending. Maybe shopping is their drug of choice, and it is used to cover up some other kind of pain. Maybe your spouse is saying hurtful things to you because you are a safe target. They may have so much built up hurt and issues with abandonment, and because they know you won't leave, the volcano has finally erupted.

Maybe the only way they know how to communicate love is through sex because someone taught them that is what love is. Maybe your spouse does not want to have sex with you because certain things during sex bring back memories of molestation. Maybe your spouse does not know how to be a good parent because they never had one modeled, or they grew up bouncing around in foster care. Maybe your spouse suffers with rage because of bad childhood experiences. Maybe things you do or say trigger hurtful memories they have from previous relationships and your spouse is suffering from some sort of PTSD.

Maybe your spouse isn't lazy, but because of the war they having going on in their mind, it is hard for them to get out of the bed every morning. They may be suffering from depression, spiritual attacks, low self-esteem, or anxiety. Maybe your spouse can't cook because nobody ever showed them how. Maybe your spouse is letting you down because you are expecting them to be what your daddy or your mother was, but they are their own individual.

If you notice all of these things could seem like personal attacks, but it is really just a result of a lack of honesty, communication, and being unaware to certain wounds or truths. You cannot have true intimacy without honesty. We mentioned that the Bible says two flesh become one. I am a firm believer that if you can't talk to your spouse about these hidden issues, dark secrets, painful memories, or you feel the need to hide, you may have married the wrong person, or you need to find some way to reach that intimacy of truth. If you know it is affecting your marriage, you really shouldn't keep it to yourself. You should never have to lie or hide something from your spouse. If you feel that you have to, it is because somewhere down the road to your marriage, you skipped some steps of laying down a godly foundation for your marriage. You must have taken a shortcut when you should have taken the longer scenic route and got to know each other a little bit better.

The solution to this problem is prayer and communication. You need the prayer because you need to ask God for the wisdom on how to say what needs to be said. If you are the one who knows you are struggling with inside issues that are affecting your marriage, you need to ask God to give you the right time and words to say to express these things to your spouse. If you are the one who is seeing something that your spouse is doing that seems wrong, you need to pray and ask God for the wisdom on how to talk to your spouse in love and not come off as accusing, belittling, or trying to bully them to see it your way. If you come across hostile, mean, or uncaring, your spouse may not feel safe sharing the very thing that is hindering your marriage with you.

You want everything that is in darkness to be brought to the light. The Bible says my people are destroyed for lack of knowledge. You keep thinking your spouse is attacking you personally, when they are really just fighting some ugly battles on the inside. You keep thinking your spouse is crazy, or they don't care about you. But, they probably seem crazy because they wish they could communicate or express their love for you, but are unable to. You think your spouse just doesn't get or love you, but the truth is you two just don't speak the same love languages. They express love through touch, but because you were molested as a child, you do not receive touch as love. They express love through gifts, but because your father always sent presents and never his presence, you don't receive gifts as love. You see it as trying to be bought or unthoughtful. They express love through sex because they desire the connection and the oneness, but because you had several sexual partners or casually had sex outside of marriage, you don't receive it as love because you don't appreciate it for the way God created it to be. They express love through just wanting to be around you all the time, but you would prefer they help clean the house or offer to do the dishes.

Many of the fights you or having or based off of misunderstanding, and assuming the other person can read your mind or thinks like you. I have had many men complain that their wives want them to be mind readers. Instead of saying what they want or what is bothering them, they just want the husband to automatically know what they want or figure out what is both erring them. I have heard wives complain that their husbands never open up or let them know how they are feeling, but they really don't know how to comfort or support their husbands. Both of these can be fixed with simple communication. If the answer is so simple, why do marriages struggle? I will talk about this in the next chapter when we talk about fighting dirty.

If you want to have a better perspective of your marriage, you need to understand that your spouse is not perfect and sometimes they will let you down. This is not a personal attack. The reason we get so offended is because our flesh is selfish, and as soon as our needs are not being met, we want to go to war. You need to know that maybe some of the expectations you have put on your spouse are expectations that only God can meet. That is why you keep getting disappointed. If you open your eyes and identify which of your expectations are unrealistic of your spouse and need to be placed in God's hands, you will take a ton of weight off of your marriage. This removes putting the power in your spouse's hands and back into yours. You must carry some of your burdens to Jesus Nobody is stopping you but you. The beautiful thing about having a spouse is that you have someone who you can confide in, and they join you in prayer on your behalf. If you put your hope in man, the disappointment will be there; if you put your hope in Jesus, He will blow your mind every time. What am I saying? You can eliminate some of the disappointment in your marriage by refocusing your eyes unto the proper source.

I am not sure men struggle with this as much because men are visual creatures, and we often chase with our eyes. But, have you ever fallen in love with someone's potential? Have you ever seen a real beautiful woman with a guy who was not going to win any awards for his looks? Why is this? Usually, she saw something about him on the inside that stole her heart. Women are good at seeing potential in a man. The problem is that they sometimes fall in love with the potential of who a man could be, but don't love the person he actually is at the moment. Some women take these as challenges. They look at that man as a project, and when he fails to ever live up to their potential, or what the woman thought he should be, they are left disappointed and bitter because of all the time and effort they wasted with this man.

Have you fallen in love with someone's potential and not them? What happens when they have the potential but no drive to go out there and do what it takes to reach it? The only way to know if your expectations are realistic is by getting to know the person better. Many people are good talkers, but can they actually walk the walk? They can sell you a dream, but is their dream realistic? Are they making any effort to achieve it? Ladies, sometimes your man may need a kick in the behind or some inspiration. Pray to God for wisdom, and ask Him to show you how to aid your man in realizing and achieving his full potential. He may not have the confidence because of verbal abuse as a child or low self-esteem. Instead of picking up were his abusers left off and cutting him down with more words, try building him up and giving him the kind of support he is not used to. This goes for the husbands as well. There are many women who think all they have to offer is sex or struggle with low self-esteem. Ask God how you can be a good example and support to your wife.

Ask God to give you directions to help unfold and show your wife the beauty, talent, ministry, and gifts Gods has put inside of her. If you belittle talk down to her, you will only cause her to withdraw more into her shell. Many times, we have realistic expectations for people, but lack the wisdom to help them achieve it. Once again, the answer to this is prayer and communication! Stop fighting dirty in your marriage and put it in God's hands. Your spouse is not your enemy, the devil is.

CHAPTER 6

Throw Some Wood on the Fire

Keeping the fire blazing, will keep both of your warm.

I f you take a hard look at yourself this past year, can you say you have truly been making an effort in your marriage, or at least the same effort you made at the start? Are you letting the fire go out in your marriage? I have always been a firm believer that the fire doesn't have to go out in your marriage no matter how long you have been together. When you first started dating, you made initial contact and felt a spark. Through dating, flirting, and talking, that spark turned into a fire. That fire made you two attracted to the warmth of it, and made you want to come together and get married. Some people just assume that with time the fire and passion will die down, and you will become used to your partner. Other people believe that the fire will just self-sustain and always be there.

Fires will die down, I don't care how in love you think you are at the start. Life happens, familiarity sets in, and you just get old. Notice I didn't say the fire dies, if you really love someone, there will always be that flicker there. You don't want to live at a flicker when you can live with a roaring fire. The biggest reason fires are reduced to a flicker is because couples build the fire then get stuck into a routine. You get lazy laying around that warm fire, and you stop gathering wood to throw into it. There will come a point in your marriage where you will have heard every story your spouse has to tell, fought about the same old stuff, had the same routine during sex, and do the same things week after week. We don't have to wait until the fire dies, and things get cold to try to spice things up. Marriage is a beautiful thing, and it can always improve, evolve, and grow if we just have the motivation, dedication, and willingness to make an effort to keep the fire alive.

If you read the story of Paul being shipwrecked on the island, you will see how there was fire on the island, and instead of him just sitting up next to it and being warm until it died, he went to gather some more wood. Do you feel like the hottest days of your marriage are behind you? Did you just ride the wave and let things die down gradually? What are you doing to keep the fire going in your marriage? If you don't have nothing new to talk about, go out and do something you have never done before at least once a month. Sometimes, we get used to our spouse because we never have a chance to miss them. Join some kind of individual activities during the week. This not only gives you a chance to miss each other, but something to talk about as well when you come back together.

If your marriage has been stale, it is probably because the both of you have been on autopilot for quite some time. You have a routine that you stick to, and this is taking the excitement and suspense out of the marriage. You always have tacos on Tuesday nights. Every Friday night, you watch Netflix or rent a Redbox DVD until you fall asleep. You always have sex twice a week at a set time. The only place you go outside of work, and the grocery store is church. This is how the fire in a marriage dies. When you were dating, it was a brand new experience. You were not sure where things were going or how you would respond to one another. When you got married, the excitement of living together and starting this brand new life together kept the fire plenty warm, but once you got used to one another's routines, habits, and had a few fights, you just kind of went into autopilot.

I want to encourage you not to wait another day to get the fire back in your marriage. Force yourself to get out of your comfort zone, and do something spontaneous, new, and unpredictable. I understand money can be tight, but everything does not cost money. Get out of the house, and do something new. Many couples like to work out together. You may want to take an aerobics or gym class together. You can try hiking or bike riding. Maybe your partner doesn't like all that physical stuff, and they enjoy something that will stimulate their mind. If you guys never go anywhere, just get in the car one weekend and drive to the next state over and explore. If you always go on the same kind of dates, research online and find a new place to try. Maybe you just need to get out of the house for a weekend and hit a hotel. Sometimes, a change of scenery can bring the spark back. Maybe you are the kind of couple who is always busy, always running, and always out of the house. Maybe you just need to slow down, cuddle in bed all day, watch movies, and order food.

Make a list of things that you can pretty much count on in your marriage. For instance, "I know every time we get paid, my husband brings home a movie and we order pizza. Maybe this time I will suggest that we get out the house and try a new restaurant." Try to break out of being repetitive and sticking to a set schedule in everything you do in your marriage. Figure out a way to surprise your spouse.

Effort is everything in a marriage. Sometimes, in order to make the effort your spouse needs, you will have to sacrifice. This is not always going to feel good, but if you want to keep the fire going, you are going to have to make the effort to gather some wood. Ask yourself what kind of wood you can gather to throw into the fire of your marriage. You husbands may want to just tell your wives to relax, and you will take care of the dishes or clean the house. From what I have learned, cleaning the house or helping with some of the chores will get your wife more excited than having big muscles. Maybe letting her sleep a little bit longer on the weekend by taking care of the kids' breakfast or taking them to the park. They like that as well. Maybe you just tell her to get in the car, and surprise her by taking her to get her nails and hair done, or just get a massage. Find out what your wife likes, or maybe something she has always wanted to do. Wait a few weeks, and then just surprise her with it one random day. These things take effort, but best believe when you throw that wood unto that fire, it will shine bright and get hot!

Ladies men are pretty simple. I know this sounds funny, but we are not complicated at all. Men like sex, food, and space. We don't even care in which order necessarily. Often times if you put in the effort to look cute, cook his favorite meal, and give him some space to watch sports or work on his hobby, he will be very glad. When polled what was most important to men and women in a marriage sex was always one of the top two things for men. We will talk about sex in a later chapter, so I will expound more on other ways you can put effort into building your fire outside of this.

Leaving a note or letter of appreciation always goes a long way to make your partner feel special. Women need to feel beautiful. They like knowing their husband is into them and appreciative of what they do. Men like to know they are needed, because of our ego. Ladies, you may just leave a note for your husband, or send him a text telling him you appreciate him going to work and providing for the family. Men, you might try leaving a romantic note telling your wife how much you adore her and look forward to seeing her every day. Let her know how beautiful she is and how much you enjoy having her in your life. You can get creative with these notes and message, and maybe add candy, balloons, and flowers; and, ladies, for your man, some sort of flirtation.

Ladies love to be romanced and made to feel special. Men like to know they are needed and that they are the big man in your life. In some marriages, just giving a compliment is an effort for some people. It is actually not normal in some marriages to complement one another. This could be because of one's childhood growing up, pride, or several other things. Whatever the reason, put it to the side and let your partner know how beautiful, wonderful, or big and strong they are. When we argue people have so many negative things to say, but just like those negative seeds can be planted, so can good ones. You should make it a point to tell your spouse something positive about themselves and how you feel toward them at least once a day.

I hear sometimes that the spouse does not want to complement their partner because they don't want them to get a big head, but, if you hold back from making a deposit your account is going to eventually be in the negative, and somebody else will always come and make a deposit. Don't be surprised when some other lady at your husband's job is telling him how handsome he is or what a good man he is. If you are never telling him, he is going to be hungry for this and happily receive it. If you never compliment your wife and tell her she is pretty, or that you appreciate her, best believe some other guy will. She may be at work, or grocery shopping, and some other guy is going to let her know how pretty she is or what a good mother she is. The only one who needs to be filling up your spouse's ego and emotional tank is you. When you build your spouse up, you make it hard for the devil to get in with bitterness and temptation. When you don't meet your spouse's needs, you make it easier for them to be susceptible to entertaining inappropriate relationships or just becoming bitter and depressed.

Ladies, remember how when you first started dating your husband you would never let him catch you slipping? You wouldn't come out the door until your hair was right, your make up was on, and your outfit was looking just right. God created men to be visual creatures. Many men struggle with pornography because of this, and some men are very shallow because they are all about how the outside looks. Many guys don't even care to get to know a woman if she looks good to them. Some of us are so foolish we get hypnotized by curves, her long hair, her cute smile or whatever it is that man likes.

Our friends can be like man that girl is crazy, but if we think she looks good enough, we will deal with it. Many guys stay in bad relationships just because they are so attracted to their wife they don't want to let her go or because they don't think they will find somebody as attractive. I know that might sound crazy to females, but you must understand that females always have men coming to them. The average guy who is not a basketball player, movie star, or model is surprised when we find out a girl likes us or we get a compliment. Ladies usually are turning down several guys' advances all week long. This is why it is very important to keep up your looks, ladies. Number one, you should want to give your husband the best version of yourself that you can. Take that time to do your hair, do some sit-ups, and do some squats or whatever it is that you need to do. I promise you, your husband will appreciate the effort. Many ladies get married and just let it all go. When your husband walks into the kitchen in the morning you are looking like his little brother. I know this sounds funny, but many women wonder why their husbands keep cheating, looking at other women, or struggling with porn, and this is one of the reasons why.

When a man sees you looking rough over and over again, not only is that a turn off, but he may feel like he is not worth the effort that you once put in anymore. Some ladies say, "Well, why should I get all dolled up if I am not going anywhere?" Remember I said before, you don't want your marriage to be quid pro qou. Sometimes, you should just do something for your spouse and expect nothing in return. You get dolled up because you love him, and you want him to have something to look at when he comes home. I can tell you firsthand, I love when my wife gets dolled up and I come home from a hard day of work. It is almost like food for my eyes. I always feel like, "Wow, today was hard, but coming home to you makes it all worth it!" Some ladies love saying, "My man should be attracted toward me regardless," but these women are usually just lazy and making excuses.

Men, you should do your best to keep up your physical appearance as well. Most women are not as concerned with this as men are, but more than likely your wife isn't blind. Give her something to look at, but don't be surprised if that fails to impress her. One of the best ways you can make an effort is to listen to her. You may not always feel like it right after work, but take the time out just to let her vent. When you walk through the door, show that you are thoughtful and ask her how her day was. Don't offer solutions or tell her how to fix issues she may bring up, just listen and be there for her. Men tend to be problem solvers, but, often times, your wife isn't looking for your solution. She is just looking for you to listen to her, and let her know you appreciate her. When you come home, and she has cooked a meal, or you both are working, offer to do the dishes, cook, or rub her feet. The biggest way you can show your wife you love her is sacrifice. If you are a Godly man, you are working like the Bible says you should and your wife will see this. She knows you are working and are probably tired, so when you come home and give her your time, energy, or go out of your way to do something special for her, she is going to appreciate it.

Everything I mentioned is just general things that work for couples, but you need to talk to your spouse and find out what they like. Everybody is unique. Don't assume what your friend did for his wife is going to work for yours, and don't assume what worked in past relationships will work in this one. Communicate with your spouse, and be prepared for them to like or want somethings that you just simply won't feel like doing all the time. I promise if you roll up your sleeves, cut down the wood, and throw it in the fire, it will blaze! When your spouse wins, you win, and you both can enjoy the warmth that comes with that big fire. Get away from doing things the same old boring way and put some effort into your marriage. You will learn new things about your spouse and see a new side of them when you change things up. It is up to you to keep the fire going in your marriage.

CHAPTER 7

My Blah Marriage

Do you have a "good" but boring marriage? Do you look at your marriage and not really have any complaints, but still feel as if something is missing? Do you feel like your marriage has peaked and is on its way down? Do you feel like the best years are far behind you? Do you ever find yourself thinking this is as good as it is going to get? Do you imagine being married to somebody else, how amazing you think that would be, and all of the things that you guys would do? Do you feel like your marriage is something you just have to put up with or survive through until you die? Do you have any expectations for your marriage's future other than paying bills, surviving, and living together?

Your perspective is everything in your marriage. I have learned during my walk with God that every day is not going to be awesome and brand new. Some days, there are just going to be mediocre, and you have to learn how to get through all those mundane days and still have joy. Every day of your marriage is not going to be a honeymoon, and it won't be awful either.

Some seasons of your marriage will just be routine life. You work, you eat, you fulfill your obligations, and go to sleep. This is actually the hardest part of marriage, and your walk with God, to get through. During these seasons, many people lose motivation and they either shrink into isolation and depression, or they try to force something to happen to make things exciting. Sometimes, you are going to have to just go with the flow. You will have to get through that Monday through Friday period just to make it to another weekend in your marriage. Just because you hit this season in your marriage does not mean your marriage is dying, or over. The reality is life is just life sometimes and you will have your highs and lows. Like a plane that is flying in the sky, you just have to learn how to level out. Notice, though, that I said season. If your marriage just seems to have been in this season forever with no change, you might have some deeper issues to work on and resolve. Don't be discouraged. Anything is possible with God.

I want to let you know that the best days of your marriage are ahead of you. I don't care what you have been through, what you have done, how the other partner is behaving, or even if you feel like your spouse can never measure up to someone else you have been with in the past. I want you to shake off these lies that are not of God. We have already made it clear that God honors marriage. Jesus didn't come down and die on the cross for us to live a mediocre, oppressed, and depressed life.

> The thief cometh not, but for to steal, and to kill, and to destroy: I am come that they might have life, and that they might have it more abundantly." (John 10:10, KJV)

God wants to breathe life into the dead parts of you. The enemy wants to steal your joy, peace, hope, and destroy your faith. Jesus wants to restore, uplift, encourage, and build up your faith. There is nothing that is impossible for God. We put limits on God because we lack faith and want things how we want them. Often, what we want and what God has for us does not line up. Many people are not willing to try in their marriage because they simply don't want it anymore. Others don't feel like doing anything new or trying to take on any new challenges because they are comfortable with where they are. Life has beaten some marriages down to the point where they are just grateful they are still together and not divorced. That is the highlight of some marriages. "We made it through another year.

We didn't get a divorce!" This is no way to live. You should expect great things for your marriage. Your marriage shouldn't be all about struggling to survive and fighting back stress and pain your whole life. God has something more for you and your spouse.

I am here to tell you God can take the worst, unloving marriage and turn it around into the best most loving marriage you ever seen. We often limit the miracles in our life because we limit God in our minds. He would love to swoop in and blow your mind away with His power and goodness, but you are sitting there with no faith. People often say they are waiting on God, but God is waiting on them. Your marriage could change if you started making the effort and change your perspective. Do you know who you are living with? Many people look at their spouse and talk them down in their minds. Do you see your spouse as God sees them? Do you see the limitless potential in their life? Many women look at their husbands and don't support his dreams or visions, or think he is just full of it. Or, maybe, you see something in him, that he does not see, but you have given up trying to help him see his potential. Many husbands look at their wives as simply caretakers. They just see a woman who takes care of the them, the kids, and the house, but in God's eyes, she is so much more. One of the reasons your marriage can seem so "blah" is because the way you look at your spouse is completely wrong. You need to ask God to open your eyes and allow you to see in them what He sees.

We talked about what God expects from husbands and wives in the previous chapters. Maybe you're in a marriage where you feel your spouse does not deserve your love or respect. Maybe you feel so miserable or have just found a way to kind of coexist in a dead marriage. You need to have the faith to trust God at His word. Even if you feel your spouse is not entitled to what the Bible commands of you, do it anyway in faith. Many people give up because they look at what their spouse or marriage is now and lose all motivation and faith.

> What *does it* profit, my brethren, if someone
> says he has faith but does not have works? Can
> faith save him? If a brother or sister is naked and

destitute of daily food, and one of you says to them, "Depart in peace, be warmed and filled," but you do not give them the things which are needed for the body, what *does it* profit? Thus also faith by itself, if it does not have works, is dead. (James 2:14–17, NKJV)

The Bible says faith without works is dead. You can say you believe the scripture all day, but, if you are not acting on it, that really means nothing. If you can be the husband or wife God has commanded you to be regardless of what your spouse is doing, this is an act of faith. This shows God that even though you don't feel like it, and you don't think it is fair, you trust God. This says, "God I know that if I obey you, you will take care of me." God cannot resist this kind of faith! He loves faith that may not make sense to anybody else. Your friends and family may be giving you the worst advice, and instead of putting your stock in what the Bible says, you put stock in what they are saying and wonder why things seem to get worse. God loves the kind of faith that says, "I don't care how it looks to anybody else, I don't care what people say about me. I am going to follow this Word and hold on to the promises of God."

When Jesus had entered Capernaum, a centurion came to him, asking for help. "Lord," he said, "my servant lies at home paralyzed, suffering terribly." Jesus said to him, "Shall I come and heal him?" The centurion replied, "Lord, I do not deserve to have you come under my roof. But just say the word, and my servant will be healed. For I myself am a man under authority, with soldiers under me. I tell this one, 'Go,' and he goes; and that one, 'Come,' and he comes. I say to my servant, 'Do this,' and he does it." When Jesus heard this, he was amazed and said to those following him, "Truly I tell you, I have not found anyone in Israel with such great faith" (Matt. 8:5–10, NIV)

Do you have this kind of faith? God has already given us the word we need, but do you believe it? Jesus was impressed with this Centurion's faith. Maybe your marriage is paralyzed, dying, or on its way down. Do you believe that God can turn it around? If your answer is yes, I want to encourage you to start showing your faith in your actions. Your spouse may not deserve your love, respect, or effort, but keep planting those seeds in faith.

> And whatsoever ye do, do *it* heartily, as to the
> Lord, and not unto men. (Col. 3:23)

Don't do it for your spouse, but do it for God. Have a made up mind that you don't care what anyone else is doing or saying, and you don't care what your situation looks like, you will obey God. This is one of the keys to unlocking blessings in your life. I want you to continue to pray, fast, and make the effort in your marriage. Remember that Jesus loves you, and He honors marriage. If you are faithful, God will work everything out. Fire is always contagious. If you keep investing passion, love, and effort into your marriage, God will bring the increase.

You may have fallen into a pattern of mediocrity. Maybe you and your spouse are good, but just bored in your marriage. Maybe you have been together so long, you feel like you are just kind of waiting for the end. I want to encourage you and tell you that any day you wake up on this side of the ground, you are blessed. You have a chance every time you open your eyes in the morning to take control of your day, your life, and your marriage. You can start turning things around right now if you are willing to put aside your pride, laziness, get out of your comfort zone, and make some sacrifices. You may have read the previous chapter and say I have been trying to throw wood on the fire of our marriage for years, but we just can't keep it going. We get a few sparks for a few months, and then fall right back into our mediocrity.

If this is the case, your marriage may not be lacking love or passion, just mission. God gave Adam a mission, then He gave him a wife as a helpmate. God created a team for a purpose. You and your spouse may need to come together and seek God for the purpose of your union. Start asking God why He put you two together and make you one. What talents, dreams, and abilities do you guys have when you combine together? So many marriages spend all of the years focusing on building a living that they never build a life. Have you guys just been living from paycheck to paycheck, job to job, year to year with no other purpose other than paying bills, providing, and making it through another year?

God put your marriage together for more than just paying bills, taking care of kids, and working until the day you die. We all have our earthly responsibilities, but what about our heavenly ones? Do you guys have a joint mission that you are carrying out for the Kingdom of God? Many people feel incomplete when they don't know who they are in Christ and what their purpose is. The same thing can happen in marriage. Many people lose their identity or put it on the back burner when they get married.

God may have called you to preach and be a pastor, but you have put that identity on the backburner in order to provided and be a father. God may have called you to lead a women's ministry, but you have forgotten about that in order to take care of your home and your children. This lack of balance could be what is causing your marriage to fall into the pit of mediocrity. Your spirit man is scream-ing inside of you that there is more to life than what you currently are experiencing. God is calling you guys deeper, but you are too caught up with the cares of this life. You are too loyal to the pattern you have become accustomed to living. You don't feel you have the energy to invest into anything else in your life right now. This may be way throwing wood in your fire is not working. You guys may have the wrong focus as to what the problem is in your marriage.

You may love each other greatly and are committed to each other, but the real problem is you focus so much on each other, that you have taken the focus off what God has for the both of you. Maybe you are doing everything the Bible says to do. You guys love each other, respect each other, and are intimate with each other, but you have just made that a pattern with no production. Your marriage should produce something. There is more to your marriage than just saying I am being a biblical spouse, and we are handling our earthly responsibilities.

You guys have a spiritual obligation and mission that comes from God. The missing piece in your marriage is a lack of assignment. When you guys learn your assignment and make moves toward accomplishing it, the joy, the fire, the passion, and the restoration will come to your marriage. The hunger inside of your marriage can only be satisfied by becoming what God has called you guys to be as a team. I promise you there is no joy in this world like walking in the purpose that God has for you. It is also an amazing feeling watching your spouse grow, step into their purpose, and knowing you were there to see it go from the birthing stage to operating as a mature adult.

CHAPTER 8

What Did You Cook Today?

You feed my eyes, but what about my soul?

While I was praying one day, God asked me what I fed my wife that day. I didn't understand it at first, but the more I prayed, God opened up my understanding. Ninety percent of the battles we fight are in our minds. If we can get away from bad thinking habits, we can overcome hard situations much more easily. Negative thinking is what causes people to be depressed, bitter, hopeless, and feel like quitting. It all starts as seeds that get planted from childhood and grow into adulthood if not corrected. There are good seeds that can be planted as well as bad ones. Which seeds are you planting and watering in your spouse? Are you helping water the good seeds that bring forth the best in your spouse, or are you watering the bad ones that bring out the worst? Do you speak life or death into your partners mind and heart. Have you ever noticed how somebody you don't care about can say something about you, but it doesn't really affect you, but if a person you love comes around and says the same exact things it can feel wonderful or even terrible depending on what they said? Your words have much power with people who love you.

You may be wondering what kind of seeds I am talking about. Imagine your spouse was told they were stupid as a child over and over again. Someone planted that seed in their mind and over time.

Even if they seem to have overcome it, that seed was planted. Do you knowingly or unknowingly damage your spouse's self-esteem by making them feel like they are not smart, making them doubt themselves, or calling them similar names? Remember, seeds produce life when watered. Whatever you choose to water in your spouse is the fruit that you will eat of later. When you plant good seeds in your spouse, you will reap when they produce good fruit. There are some things that you are going to have to deal with in your spouse that you simply didn't plant but you will have to reap. This can be a good and bad thing. If your spouse was raised right by Godly parents, you will reap the benefits of the teachings and example they set. If your spouse, for instance, had exes who broke their heart and did them wrong, you can also reap some of the negative stuff from those seeds of experiences that were planted.

When God asked me what I was feeding my wife, He was asking me what I am feeding her soul to make her better as a woman. What am I feeding her emotional and mental tanks to reinforce her best qualities and help her find new ones? To take it even further, what fruit was I giving my wife to eat of me? Was I giving her my best fruit, or was I giving her my bitter fruit? Was I showing her my best traits from seeds that had been planted in me, or showing her the ugly side? What was I picking off of the tree of my emotions, my heart, my mind, and my character to feed to my wife? Do you show the fruits of the Spirit toward your spouse?

> But the fruit of the Spirit is love, joy, peace, longsuffering, gentleness, goodness, faith, meekness, temperance: against such there is no law. (Gal. 5:22–23, KJV)

This is the beauty of two people coming together and becoming one. Maybe your spouse has seeds planted inside of them that you don't have. Maybe their parents, teachers, pastor, or grandparents instilled somethings in them that you never had planted in you. Maybe your spouse knows how to love, communicate, be a peacemaker, or has certain talents or abilities you don't have. The beauty of marriage is you can take that good seed that was planted in you, and plant it in your spouse. Maybe your spouse does not know how to be gentle and kind because everything in their life was rough, and life has made them rigid and hard. If you plant gentleness in your spouse with patience, love, and consistence, eventually, it will grow in them just like it took root and grew in you. Both of you can take what is planted in you and come together to make something so beautiful. Don't be too proud to learn and draw from each other's strengths. Share the good stuff, and work out the bad things.

The things that you have eternally can be passed between each other. Believe it or not, your spouse feeds off of you. Whatever you give them to eat will show up in their behavior and actions. Sometimes, this can be one sided and you must be long suffering. You may keep giving your spouse sweet apples, and they keep giving you spoiled berries, or nothing at all. This is where you must lean on your faith and trust the scripture.

> Do not be deceived: God cannot be mocked.
> A man reaps what he sows. (Gal. 6:7)

The Bible does not say it depends on where you sow. It says you will reap what you sow. The Bible does talk about sowing on good ground, but even if you are sowing on bad ground and your spouse is rejecting you, God can perform a miracle. He can take that hard heart and soften it. He can take that rebellious spirit and break it. Worst case scenario is you keep sowing and God removes them out of your life if they are that stubborn, and you will reap in other ways. The bottom line is you have to stick it out and obey the principle of God's word with consistency. Just because it looks like it isn't working, doesn't mean that God is not working. We often fail to realize that our blessings come disguised as burdens. When we want God to change a situation, He is often using the situation to change us.

I never got a lot of compliments and reassurance when I was a child. I grew up with just my mother and never talked to my father. This created a void inside of me that I could not really fill on my own. It made me a hard worker and always glad to get a compliment or some sign of appreciation for my work, but all that hard work to try to fill the void didn't work. I would just feel tired. So when my wife encourages me, and tells me how much she appreciates me this really makes me feel like the man! I draw strength from the compliments she is giving me. I may have a really hard day, but if my wife just leaves a small note with a compliment, or some flirtation, I get charged up and motivated because this fills that void that was inside of me. It may not seem like a big thing to you, but we have to remember that everyone is wired different. We can't project how we feel on other people. That is a recipe for disaster.

My wife had way more support and people to pour into her as a child. So, even though I feed her compliments and support, she does not feed off it as much as I do. My wife feeds more off of acts of service. When I sacrifice my time to do things for her, that fills her up more than words do. My wife has had situations where people told her things and didn't come through on what they said. So, she would rather see actions than hear words all the time. She is used to people complimenting her and being there for her with words. What she is not used to is acts of service and kindness.

You may be asking how this works. Well, if I see my wife is tired, depleted, or feeling down, I have to grab the fruit of compassion from my tree and also one of the other fruits that resulted from seeds being planted inside of me. Now, the other seeds planted in me can be my God-given talents and abilities, or things I learned along the way.

I have to identify that my wife is hungry for something. She could be starving for attention, reassurance, compliments, time, or other voids that are inside of her. I mentioned before that my wife likes acts of service. If I know my wife wanted a fence in the backyard and I have the talent planted inside of me to build one, I build it. If I don't have the talent inside of me, because the seed of hard work was planted inside of me, another seed grew from that which was income. If I can't build the fence because I lack the fruit on my tree, I can grab my other fruit of income and pay someone to do so. The effort I put into doing something to feed my wife's needs or desire will give her strength, joy, and other good qualities. She, in turn, will more than likely return the favor. The problem is we often just project our desires and ways of doing things on everyone else, and we never take the time to actually learn our spouse.

We can feed our spouse in small and big ways. Sometimes, it is just a quick "I love you," flirtation, compliment, or a listening ear. Other times, it can be a grand gesture that required time, effort, and sacrifice. What are you cooking for your spouse? Do you ever cook for your spouse? Are they always the one cooking, and serving up compliments, support, and investing in the foundation that holds your marriage together? Every day, you should be cooking up something in your mind to feed your spouse. The more you feed them, the more you nourish your marriage. The more nourishment your marriage gets, the healthier it will be for the both of you. A healthy marriage is such a beautiful thing.

Your spouse may have some fruit that you see hanging from their tree that you admire. Never be too proud to ask your spouse for advice, help, or guidance. Never become unteachable or act like your spouse has nothing to show you, or contribute. If you believe this, it is because you don't really know your spouse. God gave everyone gifts, unique personalities, and we all have something to offer this world.

If you want to know how to be gentle like them, or good at math, or good at cooking, or how they stay resilient ask them. They were fortunate enough to have somebody in their life plant the seed in them, and they can do the same for you. When you recognize each other's strengths and weaknesses, you can work together at balancing each other out. You really have to remove pride out of the equation for this to work. You cannot look down on or belittle one another. If you know your spouse is better with money, and they have the fruit to produce it, let them manage the books or ask them to show you how. If you keep trying to manage it and you don't have the skill or know how to do it, you look foolish struggling, when your spouse has the capability. You cause your marriage to be at a disadvantage when there is no reason for it to be! If you see your spouse is doing something that works better for the kids, remove your pride and learn from what they are doing. Don't sit there trying to figure out a way to outdo them, so you don't have to admit that their way worked better. This is a waste of time in your marriage. If their way works better use it, and come together as a team and see if you can cook something up together.

Marriage is teamwork, and you don't always have to cook individual dishes. You can come together and say let's just put our fruits together and cook up a love feast! You guys can plan a vacation, a getaway, take a class, or just brainstorm ways to do something together that you both will feed from. The fact is everybody has a tank and life will drain it. Some people have a little bit more in certain tanks because it was put in them early on. If you learn to work together, feed, and serve each other in humility and love, you will have an amazing life. Whatever you two cook up together, your children will feast on. You should hope that you build on what your parents gave you, eliminate the bad, become a better version of yourself, and pass it on to your children. Each generation should become better than the last if you do this correctly.

CHAPTER 9

Sex Inside of Marriage

As a loving hind and a graceful doe,
Let her breasts satisfy you at all times;
Be exhilarated always with her love.

—Proverbs 5:19

I know many men couldn't wait to get to this chapter and a few ladies as well. Some of you may have skipped all the other chapters, and said, "Baby, let's read this one first!" If that is the case, stop here and return to the first chapter. I know some of you are wondering why I posted that particular verse as the opening to the chapter. I only did so to show that even though many churches shy away from the topic of sex, the Bible doesn't. I believe the church should speak about it more often in the appropriate setting of course.

Sex plays a very important role in marriage, but if you live the kind of life we talked about in the preceding chapters, sex really won't be as big a problem in your marriage. Because of that, I left this chapter more toward the end of the book. I have learned that a marriage built on the foundation of sex alone is bound to fall and struggle, but at the same time, a marriage without it is guaranteed to almost always die sooner or later. When people tell me sex in marriage isn't that important, I always ask them why does cheating sexually make people more mad than almost anything else in a marriage that goes bad? Sex is very important and very powerful.

At the same time, you need more than sex to keep a marriage together. In marriage, you have all the time in the world to really get to know each other's body and build some sexual chemistry, but at the same time after having so much sex, you will have somedays that are better than others. Some seasons that are more passionate than others and so forth.

If all you guys had to keep your relationship or your marriage going was sex, you are going to have a very hard time. Men may not see the problem with this but some women will. What are you going do after the honey moon phase, and you have to live together? How will you connect on the days that you don't feel like having sex? What else is good about your relationship other than the sex? Banking on keeping a marriage together based on sex alone is like banking on keep the fire because of looks. Youth and looks will fade away. You got to find another way.

There have been many surveys done about marriage problems and things that people face. One particular survey I read showed that more than 90 percent of married men complained about the amount of sex they were getting. When asked to list their biggest concerns about the marriage, lack of sex was always in the top three. I know many ladies may think men are disgusting or that is pathetic, but you must realize God created men differently than you. Men and women are not wired the same. That is one of the biggest problems in marriage, projecting how you personally feel about something on to your spouse and expecting them to feel the same, or thinking how they feel or what they feel is wrong.

When I talk about this topic, I am going to speak in general, but we know that there are always exceptions to the rule, and that sometimes it can be the other way around.

For the most part, men tend to need sex a lot more than women do. We often see comedy television shows where the woman is holding out, or the man is actually very surprised when his wife is the one who initiates sex. Most women in marriage like to be flirted with, talked sweetly to, romanced, foreplay, and have the mood set before engaging in sex. Maybe at the start of the marriage, you guys are just so infatuated with each other you can't keep your hands off of each other, but eventually things normally slow down.

If you talk to most women, their sexual experience is much better when their mind is stimulated and they feel loved. Most men can just see our wives walk out the shower, brush her teeth, vacuum, sleep, yell at us, eat, or pretty much anything, and we are ready for sex! Doesn't take much foreplay or sweet words to get us going. Married women often talk about how when their husband does the dishes or helps clean around the house, that gets their engines started. For men, our engine is pretty much always started, but just on idle. Remember, I am talking about sex inside of marriage. Some of you may read this and be thinking my engine is always going as well, and you believe it always will be, but things change with age and marriage over time.

> Now concerning the matters about which you wrote: "It is good for a man not to have sexual relations with a woman." But because of the temptation to sexual immorality, each man should have his own wife and each woman her own husband. The husband should give to his wife her conjugal rights, and likewise the wife to her husband. For the wife does not have authority over her own body, but the husband does. Likewise the husband does not have authority over his own body, but the wife does. (1 Cor. 7:1–40, ESV)

I simply want you to understand that in general there is a difference between a man's and woman's level of desire to have sex once you have been married for a while. This means, husbands, you have to be patient, but, wives, you can't defraud your husband either. If the situation is vice versa, it still applies. Remember, marriage is all about serving your partner. Even though you don't want it or need it, you should want to take care of the person that you love within reason. This is biblical principle, and if you follow it, you can never go wrong. You may not understand your partners frequent desire to have sex, but they in turn might not understanding some of the things you desire or do. The reality is in marriage, there is going to be a give and take. If you are a selfish person, you won't have a good marriage. Great marriages aren't built with selfish people. When you marry someone, you are vowing to pretty much go to them with your God-given needs and only them. There are plenty of other people who could help you with your needs, but your choosing to exclusively put your desires being met in the hands of the person you choose to marry.

> Drink water from your own cistern, flowing water from your own well. Should your springs be scattered abroad, streams of water in the streets? Let them be for yourself alone, and not for strangers with you. Let your fountain be blessed, and rejoice in the wife of your youth, a lovely deer, a graceful doe. Let her breasts fill you at all times with delight; be intoxicated always in her love. (Prov. 5:15–19, ESV)

Before I get into the really deep stuff, I felt led to discuss the basics in this chapter. Your sex life may not have some of the more serious issues I am going to talk about later. It could be a simple thing like not having the energy because you don't workout. One quick way to spice up your love life is exercise. You will actually find that when you workout, there are chemicals that get released inside of your brain that make you feel good. Exercise will put you in a better mood, and also give you more energy. If you actually make the commitment to working out long enough to see real results, you will see that your desire for sex will increase as well. Many people don't feel like sex because they don't feel like doing "all of that." The fact is many people don't do much in terms of cardio and the thought of doing anything that will get their heart rate up discourages them. Also, sex is a good way of working out, be active during sex, and let your body get a workout.

Another quick way to spice up your sex life is a change of scenery and a break from routine. Many married couples get used to having sex on a schedule. Every Tuesday at 8:00 p.m., they know they are going to have sex, and they have an actually pretty good idea of the routine. If you don't have kids or even if you do, try having sex in a different room in the house, or just go get a hotel for once. Instead of sticking to the same old moves, go online to a clean site, or check out a clean book on new things you guys can try together in bed. Don't be too lazy or selfish to make the extra effort to try something different. Without having to drag this out, find ways to break out of having routine sex like it is a chore, and become more spontaneous. Nothing will drive your husband crazier than surprising him one night by being all dolled up and initiating sex. Husbands, nothing would drive your wife crazier than you actually romancing her before just jumping into the act. Set the mood with some music, candles, flowers, or whatever else you can think of. Either way, the effort both of you put into it will be appreciated and likely spark the fire and passion within. Break out of your normal. When you first get married, most couples can have the fire making love in the same bed, looking at the same walls and the same dresser, and nobody cares. But after a while, just changing up the scenery can spice things up in a hurry. At the bare minimum, maybe change the curtains and get some new sheets.

Some people will argue that sex is not a big deal in marriage or that it shouldn't be, but, if that is the case, why does it hurt so badly if your partner was to have sex with someone else? That is typically viewed as the worst thing you can do to your partner is physically cheat on them. The reason this is, is because sex is powerful. A lot more is happening during sex than just physical feelings in the body. There is a spiritual connection that takes place. Your spirits and your bodies are becoming one. Sex is not just some casual thing that you use to get a quick high. I want you to understand that everything God created has purpose, and sex has more purpose than just feeling good and reproduction.

God took a rib out of Adam and used it to create Eve. A part of Adam was inside of Eve. God said that the two flesh became one! When Adam engaged in sex with Eve, he became one with the part of him that was inside Eve. He became whole again. Your wife has a part of you inside of her that will make you a whole man. That is why she is your help mate. This is why you can't go around having sex and becoming one with just anybody. When you have sex with someone, a part of them is added to you and a part of you is given to them. Many people go around becoming one with several people, and this can cause spiritual schizophrenia.

You wonder why you are having mood swings, struggling with temptations, or have feelings like anger or depression and you never have before. When you have sex, you are opening your body and your soul to someone. You are making a supernatural connection. This is why people love make up sex. You can forgive each other with words, but it is an amazing feeling to reestablish that connection once an argument or disagreement has pulled you in separate ways. This is why sex is also better once you have had a chance to miss each other for a time. Yes, your body loves the feeling, but there is a powerful connection, restoration, and strength that comes during this act of intercourse. Believe it or not, sex is an act of worship. Whenever God's creation does something the way that He designed it, that obedience to God is worship.

Do you know the enemy would love for you and your spouse to stop having sex? Do you know that when you argue, the last thing the enemy wants to see is for you guys to make peace and have sex? The last thing he wants to see is you guys come back together and strengthen the bond. He knows that in a marriage with no sex, doors are open. The doors can be emotional or physical needs, but he can use these to lead us into sin.

> Do not deprive one another, except perhaps by agreement for a limited time, that you may devote yourselves to prayer; but then come together again, so that Satan may not tempt you because of your lack of self-control. (1 Cor. 7:5 ESV)

When a husband and wife come together and have sex, you are worshipping God and making the devil upset. The devil wants to destroy anything that God created. He does this by trying to pervert it. That is why you have homosexuality and people committing fornication, adultery, rapes, and molestation. God never designed sex to be used in any of these ways, and it is sin.

I mentioned ways to spice up your sex life earlier, but, sometimes, there are much deeper issues going on that prevent the passion from being sparked in a marriage. Sometimes, it is because of things we have done, but one of the most common things a marriage's sex life can suffer from is usually something many experience that they didn't have the power to stop. This can go either ways, but most of the time, it is the woman who is struggling with these issues inside of the marriage.

The sad thing is statistics say that as many as three out of every five women will have experience some type of molestation or rape. If you factor in that most people in our society do not believe in not having sex before marriage, a lot of women come into relationships damaged sexually. Yes, the men do as well, but, before you get turned off by what I am saying, let me explain. Men usually are not affected by sex the same way as women, nor is the percentage of men being sexually abused as high. This is why you can see a man who has a beautiful wife sleep with a woman who is less attractive and not think or feel anything about it. I have seen many men sleep around just because it was something different. I have seen guys who have been married for years have a one night stand with a female just because it was available. Often, if a woman is caught cheating, she usually has developed some type of emotional bond with the man she is having an affair with. Like I said, this is not always the case, but more than likely because of how we are wired differently it is. Very rarely will you find a woman who has a good husband and is happily married cheating just because something was available to her.

When a woman is molested or raped, she is forced into something that she does not want. She feels like her power has been stripped from her, and she has been used. During marriage, many women sometimes feel the freedom to express their power to say no. It is not a personal attack against her husband every time. Sometimes, it just feels good for her to be able to say no, when she never was able to during the molestation or rape she experienced in her past. Often times, when women go through this, they either become rigid and hard or very promiscuous. Sometimes, it can even be a combination of both. Hopefully, as a husband, you have not had to deal with her being promiscuous outside of your marriage, but many husbands do have to deal with a wife who is hardened from what she has been through. You may find yourself working twice as hard to connect with her. They key thing to help keep your mind at ease is to always remember it is not a personal attack against you. Your wife just needs healing. You must love her, be supportive, and patient throughout this experience.

Your wife may have fits of anger that often seem to be set off by the smallest of things. Before you are going to have sex, or when she knows you are trying to be intimate, she starts a fight. This could be because she is experiencing triggers that bring back painful memories. The act of sex or foreplay make take her mind back to a traumatic experience that she does not want to relive. She may not be rejecting you, just trying to protect herself from reliving the bad memory. Obviously, because men have a strong God given desire for sex, this can cause problems within the marriage. You may feel like acting distant, and some men may be even tempted to have affairs, or look at pornography. I would encourage all men to get their wives into counseling so that they can heal from their wounds.

Understand that your wife may not be comfortable talking to you about it because of shame or fear of being judged. Don't be offended by this, just pray for her and ask God to restore what is broken inside of her. I have seen many men who have had wives who physically abuse them out of fits of rage. Some men just endure it and never address it, and some men eventually physically hurt their wives back. The answer is prayer and counselling. Ladies, if you know you are struggling with this, and it is affecting your marriage, be honest with your husband. The longer you keep it hidden, the longer the enemy can continue to poke away at your marriage through those wounds.

Many women have a disgusted perspective when it comes to sex and men in general because of what they were exposed to as a child or adult. They look at sex as being used. Often times, they are turned off and can't appreciate a man's efforts because, in their mind, they think that the man is not doing this out of love, but because he wants to use them for sex. We mentioned that some women become promiscuous and this can also affect your marriage. When a woman has dealt with men over and over again who have sold her a dream or had sex with her and left, she feels used. Like it or not, there are many dogs out there who tell women what they want to hear just in order to get another notch on a belt. This can be devastating for a woman and can also be damaging in a marriage later on if not addressed.

Through counseling, prayer, and this book, you must understand and learn that your husband is not any of those men who hurt you in your past. When we get hurt in a certain area and someone comes to us and tries to draw from that area, we often reject them because we feel the wound all over again. Your husband deserves your body, just as you deserve his. Those other men may have lied to you, used you, and done many other awful things, but focus on the good qualities about your husband. Focus on what the Bible says about sex and know your husband is a different person. Don't expect your husband to heal your wound or for you to just dance around it for the rest of your marriage and expect your husband just to put up with it. You must talk about it and have it addressed so you can heal. You may not feel comfortable talking to your husband about it, and that is perfectly fine, but find a counselor, a pastor, or someone senior to you who can actually help you heal and overcome the lies the enemy has placed in your head.

I said before that it does not always have to be the woman in this predicament, it can very well be the other way around, but in most cases as statistics show, it is usually the woman struggling with this. If it is the other way around, the same solution applies. Pray to God to restore what was broken and stolen from you. Pray to God to break away the soul ties that were formed when you were in sin, or being taken advantage of. Pray to God for a healing on your perspective, so you are able to see sex the way He designed it to be and not the way sin or abuse has made you see it.

Sex plays a huge part in having a successful marriage. Many may not like to hear that or feel that is unromantic, but that is very well the problem in most marriages. People come in with a false perspective or a romanticized idea of what marriage is. There is a reason God designed sex only for marriage, and everything outside of it is a sin. Sex is a tool that restores and keeps a bond of oneness strong between a husband and wife. Sex is a tool that humbles you and makes you have the heart of a servant through taking care of one another when you don't always feel up to it. Have you ever notice your husband in a bad mood and you decided to invite him into your wonderland? What happens? Do you notice the change in him afterwards?

Men, has your wife ever been in a bad mood and you just swept her up in your arms and laid her in your bed for some romance, and she acts like a brand new person afterwards? I know this may sound funny, but it is very true. I understand all marriages are different, but the fact is God designed sex for marriage. It is designed for more than just feeling good and reproducing. I would go as far to say those are secondary to what God originally created sex for. Having sex is really the actual marriage if you look at the book of Genesis. The paper certificate is something men came up with, but the actual marriage is when the two flesh become one.

> The man said, "This is now bone of my bones, And flesh of my flesh; She shall be called Woman, Because she was taken out of Man. For this reason a man shall leave his father and his mother, and be joined to his wife; and they shall become one flesh. And the man and his wife were both naked and were not ashamed. (Gen. 2:23–25)

If your sex life is struggling or you guys just don't have the fire, the connection, or the chemistry, pray about it. There is nothing wrong with praying about your sex life. God can turn up the heat in your bedroom quickly! It is not His will for you to have a miserable marriage, and if sex is one of the areas that needs some work, just like with any other area of your marriage, God can perform a miracle.

I close this chapter with this statement. Marriage is all about serving each other. The reality of marriage is that most men communicate love through sex. Whether a woman wants to accept this or not, that is a fact. You may want your husband to show you love in other ways, and that is perfectly understandable and fine, but do not discount sex because the enemy has destroyed your view on it or because it is not your love language. Sex, or the power of touch, is a big communicator of love for men. On the flipside of that, men need to understand that you must find other ways to communicate your love for your wife. Discuss what your love languages are and make the effort to exhibit those things to one another. Whether it is doing the dishes, cleaning the garage, taking the kids, compliments, flirtation, being a listener or having sex, serve one another, and do it in love. The more you sow, the more you will reap. If you take anything from this chapter, do not project how you feel about something as the rule for your marriage. How you feel doesn't mean that it is always true. Work with each other and work on each other, if you know what I mean.

CHAPTER 10

Taking Off the Mask

*You will never know if they really love you, if you never
take off the mask and let them see the real you.*

I want to spend a little bit more time expanding on the power of
honesty in a marriage. It is hard to have true intimacy if you are
not being honest with one another. Marriage is a partnership
and there is a bond between the two of you. If you have the kind of
marriage where you can be transparent with each other, it will make
that bond even stronger. We talked about being honest at the start of
a relationship earlier. When we first start dating, we are meeting that
person's representative and they are meeting ours. Most of the time,
people don't show too much of the side of them you don't want them
to see because they want to impress you. It is good starting off your
marriage by talking about struggles, flaws, and areas you are weak in.
It is also a good idea to talk about wounds you may have received and
are not fully recovered from. The reason I say this is because they will
affect your partner in the marriage.

I struggled with trusting women because of past relationships
I was in. Any time I started talking to a new girl, in the back of my
mind, I always found myself thinking, *She must be lying to me about
something.* Because of what I have been through, I had these walls
up around my heart. I had come to believe that all women were liars
and manipulators. Of course, this is not the truth, but because of

what I went through, I had serious issues with trusting a woman or letting my walls down. This is something that I needed to be honest about before jumping into marriage. Not being honest about this would cause problems in my marriage if it showed up in my behavior. I needed to heal, and I also couldn't hold what somebody else did against my new found relationship.

The problem is sometimes, we think we are healed, but when we get into a new relationships, some things in our life can resurface. We might act in a certain way because of an old wound, and the best thing to do is just come clean and be honest. This will allow your spouse to have a better understanding and show you more patience. The person you are with might not understand certain things you do, or maybe they triggered flashbacks unknowingly and the way you reacted caused damage to them. Remember the saying hurt people hurt people? You can't keep on this image that there is nothing wrong. You obviously need counseling and healing, but it will help the new person you are with be more patient with you knowing what you have been through.

If you try to just wear a mask and act like everything is okay, eventually, you will get tired and either explode or withdraw. It is hard work to put a mask on every day and suppress everything that is going on inside of you or around you. You can never conquer what you don't address.

You leave room for confusion when you are constantly triggered by something and you refuse to explain why to the person you are with. You can't expect someone to understand, when there are so many everyday normal things that a person can do that could actually trigger a bad memory for a you. So while they are just being normal, you are actually behaving in a unhealthy manner because of the wounds or issues you carry. If you try to put a mask on, and never explain what is going on, you could damage your marriage.

When I communicate with my spouse as my partner and tell her when she does or says certain things, it triggers something inside of me that I am still healing from, it makes it easier for us to work as a team in love, as opposed to her thinking it is a personal attack, or I am just being moody toward her. The same thing applies with what we talked about in the previous chapter with molestation, or rape. Be honest with your spouse and work together to strengthen each other and love each other through it. If you don't take off the mask, your actions can be read wrong. Your spouse could feel rejected or attacked, when the truth is you love them and you just got issues that need healing.

Marriage is a partnership. I want to say that over and over again. If you had two guys working as partners for a firm, and one of them had information that could damage the company, don't you think it would only be fair to let his partner know? Maybe, you as one partner, are looking at the problem and you have no solutions. You are trying to figure it out all on your own without involving your partner. Every time you guys have a meeting or a sit down, you put on this mask like everything is handled and going smoothly, but the more the numbers begin to crash, and you see signs of your company going down, the more stressed you become.

The good thing about being honest with your partner instead of hiding the information that is damaging your company is that they may have a solution to the problem. Sometimes, when we take off the mask and are honest with our partners, we find out they may have an answer or a new perspective on the issue that we never thought of. Marriage should be 50/50 with both partners putting in the same amount of effort. Unfortunately, this rarely happens. But the fact remains that your partner has ideas, experiences, knowledge, talents, and abilities that you just don't have. You are losing out on half of your power by not including your partner on what the problem is. When you have a relationship where you can face problems together with love and honesty, you have twice the power, twice the prayers, twice the brain storming, and twice the effort being fed into find a solution. This takes tremendous pressure off of you from wearing your mask.

Your marriage can be affected by your mood. You are feeling stressed out, depressed, or angry because you are trying to fight everything on your own. Remember, whatever affects you, affects your partner, and eventually will affect your family as a unit. Your mood, whether good or bad, will be contagious, and, if no one has a clue as to why there is a mood, there will be added on stress because now there is also confusion.

I know sometimes we don't want to tell our partner things because of pride. We want to seem like we have it all together. Sometimes, we don't want to be honest with our partner for fear of being judged or looked upon as weak. Maybe the problem is a result of you not being honest before. You feel like if you come clean now, your partner will be disappointed in you. This is why I said it is always good to be honest at the start of a relationship; you give your partner the power of choice. They get to choose whether this is something they want to deal with and help you overcome, as opposed to finding out after marriage and feeling tricked and trapped. Regardless, this is no reason to continue on in your relationship wearing a mask. If you don't feel comfortable or strong enough to take the mask off, start with counseling or your pastor, and eventually include your spouse. If your problem is affecting you, remember it is affecting everyone in your house in some form. The most selfish thing you can do in your marriage is continue to wear the mask. Take it off, be vulnerable, and put it all in God's hands.

People and marriages are always evolving. As a husband, maybe things have not been going so well on your job. You don't feel like stressing your family out so you put on a mask and act like everything is ok. This may be fine if the problem only persist for a short period of time, but if it is a drawn out situation and you are starting to feel the pressure build up, take off the mask, and go to your spouse. You are not helping anyone by coming in the door every night in a bad mood, or exploding on your spouse or children because all the patience you had was used up just trying to make it through the day at your job.

Let your spouse know that you are worried about your job security, providing, and the future and let them assist you in carrying the burden. Sometimes, there may not be much that they can do, but just saying, "Hey, everything is going to be okay," or, "you know, we are here for you no matter what," can help relieve some of the pressure. Your spouse may even sacrifice some of their time or what they have going on just to cater to your stress until you get back feeling strong.

I know as men we don't want to let our family down and the weight of that can be very draining, but, if your wife really loves you, she is going to support you and be there for you at your lowest moments. We take on added stress because of fear. We worry that if we present this problem to our partner, there will be some repercussions.

With the wife, it can be very similar. We evolve, and we grow. Maybe you don't want to stay home and you want to get a job. Maybe you don't want to work anymore, and you want to stay home. Maybe the kids have gone off to school, and you are not used to not having anyone to take care of. Maybe your boss has been getting on your nerves. You may have a promotion, a demotion, or just a new way of thinking that you want to explore because of something you saw, or a conversation you had. Many times, we can find ourselves putting on a mask because we fear how change will affect the family. Instead of exploring, stepping out, or embracing that big change you feel, you shut it all down. When your husband comes home and he asks how your day was, something inside of you tells you to tell him about your new idea or new dream you want to pursue, but, because you don't feel he will support it, make time for it, agree with it, you just shut it down on the inside. This is kind of like committing an emotional suicide. That change that is trying to come forth in you is being strangled because of your fear of how your partner will receive it.

To be honest, maybe it does need to be strangled and killed. Not everything we feel is always a good thing, but that is why you should bring your partner in on it to put a second set of eyes and ears on whatever it is that is going through your mind. Often times, people put on the mask and smile, but, behind that mask, they are dying a little inside every day. Behind that mask, they are committing a murder inside. This eventually goes one or two ways. Some people get distant and depressed and they withdraw. They may get so depressed they can't even get out of bed anymore. They sit there and fantasize about being someone else, being somewhere else, and eventually the bitterness infects the whole house. Other people have a fighter attitude and they explode. They don't communicate or compromise. They just make demands, and, if those demands are not met, they unleash a world of emotional or physical pain. In both cases, the mask comes off slowly or abruptly, but not wisely. Eventually, your partner is going to see that you are depressed, or they are going to be on the bad side of an explosion.

The key here is to find the right time to take off the mask. You must use wisdom when you choose to take off the mask and expose yourself to your partner. Don't go taking off your mask and talking about something you've been holding in when your partner comes to you dealing with their own issues. This will cause them to feel rejected, and in turn- reject you. This will make you feel like never taking off the mask again, or that your partner does not care about you. This is not the case; you simply removed your mask at the wrong time. Don't take off your mask in the heat of an argument because often times, you will end up trying to wound your partner instead of finding a resolution to the problem. It is all about knowing your spouse and having a general idea of when is a good time to bring up the issue. When your spouse is relaxed and there is love in the air, it is usually the best time. Don't go busting into the room, or storming down to the couch after you guys have not been talking for two days, or there is lots of tension in the air.

If you are incapable of finding a good time to remove your mask, or you just feel like what you are hiding behind your mask is just too much, and it will destroy your marriage, get a third party involved. I always suggest going to your pastor. You want to find someone you both mutually respect because people tend to act more civil when there is someone who they want to impress around. If you have the conversation one on one, it may turn into a shouting match, someone walking away, or someone even getting physically abused. If you bring in that third party, your spouse may feel angry, sad, or want to argue, but more than likely, they will restrain those emotions because someone else is involved. They will actually put on the mask we all put on in society. If you notice, everyone acts differently at home. We don't act the same way at home as we would at our job or church. If you know your spouse always likes to dominate every conversation and you can't ever get a word in, which is why you put on your mask, get a third party involved whom they respect, and they will more than likely respect you and let you talk. If they don't, that third party can play referee and let them know when it is your turn to speak.

The beautiful thing about marriage is seeing the best and worse in a person and choosing to love them anyway. You shouldn't have to wear a mask to bed every night. You shouldn't have to wear a mask every time you engage in sex with your partner. You shouldn't have to wear a mask when your spouse comes home every day or when you are the one coming through the door. Grab your spouse by the hand, look them in the eye, take off the mask and kiss them, love them, no matter what you see. The fact is none of us are perfect. None of us have all of the answers. When two people can come together and love through it all, it is a testament of how Jesus loves us. Take off the mask of perfection, self-righteousness, and pride, and just be vulnerable and honest. You will get so much more out of your marriage when you do this. We often never reach our full potential in life because we never address what is holding us down. When we address the issue, we can overcome it, and when we can overcome it, we can move on to higher levels. Don't waste another day living behind a mask. Take it off, and let love do the rest.

> The Bible says love conquers all, "Above all, love each other deeply, because love covers over a multitude of sin" (1 Pet. 4:8).

CHAPTER 11

Sticking To My Guns

Blessed are the peacemakers,
for they will be called children of God.
—Matthew 5:9, NIV

Many times, we can be set in our ways. I have often heard people say, "This is just the way I am." "If they don't like it that's just too bad." "That's not my personality, I just don't function like that." I want you to understand that just because you have been a certain way your whole life does not make it right, nor does it always make it wrong. If your husband likes physical touch and affection, you cannot neglect this just because this does not match your personality type. This is where sacrifice and true love really comes into play. Instead of sticking to your guns and saying, "Look, this is who I am, I am not going to change, get used to it," you need to put the guns down and make peace.

Often times, there will be conflict when a person is at your mercy for their needs to be met. Maybe you are an introvert, and you really don't like going out and socializing much, but your spouse is the exact opposite. When you choose to stick to your guns, you always have to have it your way. Your spouse may suggest that they want to go on an outing with some friends, but, because of your personality, you reject that idea. If your spouse pushes the subject, you get to blasting away. This can be very damaging to your marriage. If your spouse wants to go out and socialize, you must get over being selfish. I am not saying that you have to do what your spouse wants all the time, but you should want to at least compromise. Put your guns down and say, "You know what? I will give it a try." People who selfishly stick to their guns will almost certainly have a miserable marriage.

Many times, people are a certain way because that is what they were exposed to or certain situations in life shaped their personality. When you get married, you have two different personalities coming together as one. So, yes, maybe that is not how your personality is, but if you love a person, sometimes, you will have to adapt and change in order for the marriage to flourish and blossom. Also, you can't assume because you are the type of person that doesn't need compliments or affirmation, that your spouse shouldn't need it or belittle them for needing it. Some people can be so selfish in a marriage that they believe the whole marriage revolves around how they feel. They often use forms of abuse to get what they want or to get out of doing something they don't want. Men often use the money to be in control and get their way and women often use sex. Both of these are a form of abuse. You cannot punish your spouse for having certain feelings that contradict with your personality or what your priorities are.

If you and your spouse are really in love, seeing each other compromise to meet each other's needs will only strengthen your bond. I know every time my wife does something for me that I know she didn't feel like doing, it makes me want to sow into her even more. When you sow love, sacrifice, or peace, you will eventually get it in return. This principle goes far beyond just meeting each other's needs or trying to cater to each other's personalities.

Maybe you are a very proud person, and it is hard for you to apologize when you are wrong. Maybe you are so proud that you can visually see you hurt your spouse and you still don't apologize. Maybe you even get disgusted when they are hurt, and you think they are weak, because when you think about everything you have been through, you wonder why they can't just toughen up. People like this often project their life on other people and judge them by it.

Your spouse can get mad at you for something that seems silly to you, but their background is completely different from yours. "Why are you upset that I ate the last piece of cake? When I was growing up, we didn't even have dessert in our house, and I never get upset." The fact of the matter is your spouse is not you and has not been through what you have been through. They might not be bad about the actual cake, but they may feel you were inconsiderate or even invaded a personal space that is off limits. You might be quick to think, that is silly, but remember your spouse isn't you. Respect how they feel.

People are often different because of their experiences, but just because they respond differently to something, does not make them less of a person. A person who sticks to their guns will often look at their spouse hurting or in need and think to themselves, *They will get over it.* This is pride, self-righteousness, laziness, or selfishness talking. One of these things is fueling you and preventing you from dropping your guns and saying, "I am going to comfort them. I am going to apologize. I am going to try to be more understanding of how they are feeling." Everybody can be guilty of this in marriage, but the thing is, once you recognize you are doing it, drop your guns.

I have often seen my wife do stuff or respond to things in a way that is different than me. I have been irritated, upset, and even angry during some of these times. What I realized is that I may not understand everything about my wife, but, at the end of the day, she is her own person. She had a life before me, different parents, different upbringing, and different experiences. I cannot force her to be like me, respond like me, or do things my way. I have to respect the fact that she is her own person. Instead of keeping my guns on her, I must set them down, love her, and always be willing to compromise.

Maybe your husband really likes sports, and he just can't wait to go to a basketball game. The thing about his interests is, sometimes, he wants you to come with him and enjoy it. He does not want to go alone. He does not want you to come along and kill the mood. He just wants you to go along and share a moment that is special to him. Believe it or not, some people have the mentality of "if I got to go to this game, I am just going to let it be known how miserable I am. I am going to complain every chance I get, I am going to pull out my cell phone and ignore everything that is going on around me." This is not love. This is not right. This is how doors are left open for the enemy to attack your marriage. Don't assume that your spouse is incapable of being tempted. Don't assume just because they are a believer that it could never happen to you. Believe it or not, if your spouse has needs and desires, you should want to fill them and help them accomplish them. You should want to give your spouse the best life they could have on this earth. You should want them to be happy and be the best version of themselves. If your mission is to be selfish in life, and have the world revolve around you all the time, you should just remain single.

If you think you are going to get into a marriage and not have to change anything about your personality, or at least modify it, you are not ready to be married. I don't care how much chemistry you have, eventually, there will be some things that you simply just don't agree on, and some interests that you simply just don't share. Many people take their spouse for granted. They stick to their guns and never expect to be shot back.

What I mean by this is they have this mindset, "I am not going to compromise, I am not going to change so you just have to deal with it. If you press my buttons, I am going to shoot my guns at you and make you pay." In their mind, they don't expect to ever be wounded back. They say, "You know what? Just go to the basketball game by yourself because I hate sports. You know what? Just go to the crafts store by yourself because I don't feel like leaving the house." When this kind of selfish behavior is repeated, you are leaving your spouse wide open. To me, this is the equivalent of a cop or a soldier having one another's back when in a hostile situation. You make your husband go to his sports events alone, and while he is there, he meets some other women. They start off innocently talking about the team, they exchange numbers, and the next thing you know, they are going to the games together all the time. You may be so selfish as to think, *Well, he should have known better, he should have never done that.* But, the fact is none of us are above being tempted. He had a need that you neglected, and it left a void inside of him.

Now, obviously, the godly thing to do would be for him to go pray about it and ask that God gives you a change of heart, but the reality is that this does not always happen. You kept your guns up, and ended up getting shot during the standoff. Same thing goes for husbands. Your wife tells you she would like for you to listen to her more or compliment her more, but you are so sleepy and never make time for her. You refuse to get over yourself and do what it takes to make your wife happy. Next thing you know, there is some guy always asking her about her day at work or when she goes shopping at the grocery store. Before you know it, your wife is going to the grocery store six times a week. It might start off as her just innocently having conversation, but once her emotional need for connection is being met, it could turn into something more. By you sticking to your guns, you left your wife vulnerable.

Many people will brush this off and say, "Well, if that is the case, I shouldn't be with them anyway." This is such lazy and selfish thinking. The fact is, if you had never left that door open in your marriage, nothing would have happened, but you were too lazy, too proud, or too selfish to get over yourself and make a change or an effort. If you are not going to fight for your marriage, what is the point of even getting married? If you have no fight in you, what does that say about your love? A person will fight for what they love, just like a person will save money for something they really want.

I have seen so many marriages end in divorce or with someone getting cheated on just because someone refused to put their guns down. I know in one relationship I was in, my partner was asking me for forgiveness for something they did to hurt me. They humbly told me they were sorry and that they wanted to work things out. They literally begged me. I know this was hard for them because they were very proud. They laid their guns down, but I kept mine up. My pride was like, "No, I am not going to forgive you. I need to make you pay for what you did to me." This left them vulnerable with their guns down and mine up and she eventually cheated on me. In a moment of weakness and vulnerability and feeling rejected, another man was able to get his foot in the door. I created a void by refusing to put my guns to the side and forgive.

It takes faith to put your guns down. You have to remember scriptures like the ones posted below. When you think about the scriptures, it helps you to have the freedom to put down your guns, and know that if you do it with the right heart, God will always take care of you and fight your battles at the end of the day.

> For the battle is not yours, but God's. (2 Chron. 20:15)

> So in everything, do to others what you would have them do to you, for this sums up the Law and the Prophets. (Matt. 7:12)

> Do not take revenge, my dear friends, but leave room for God's wrath, for it is written: "It is mine to avenge; I will repay," says the Lord. (Rom. 12:19)

> Blessed are the peacemakers, for they will be called children of God. (Matt. 5:9)

I know there are some situations in which you may feel like you need to keep your guns up in order to protect yourself or to not be taken advantage of, but if you do things with the right heart, God will always take care of you. Many times, we fear putting our guns down because we see our partner has their guns pointed at us. We find ourselves in this standoff that is doing nothing but creating tension in the home. Often times, if we would simply put our guns down and speak in love instead of hurling insults or threats, we would get a better response.

> A gentle answer turns away wrath, but a harsh word stirs up anger. (Prov. 15:1)

> On the contrary: "If your enemy is hungry, feed him; if he is thirsty, give him something to drink.

In doing this, you will heap burning coals on his head." (Rom. 12:20)

There is a very good chance that if you put down your guns, you will get shot or taken advantage of, but this is why we have the power of prayer. Sometimes, marriage is not 50/50. Sometimes, you have one person giving seventy and the other giving thirty. I have seen some marriages where one person is giving a hundred and the other is giving nothing, and if it wasn't for the one person giving 100 percent, the marriage would have been over a long time ago. God is a just God, and He has a way of bringing balance. You don't have to put your guns on your spouse and try to intimidate them into doing things your way. You don't have to make threats or deliver ultimatums. All you need to do is follow what the word of God asks of you. If you are the only one being a peacemaker all the time, and you wish for once your spouse could be the one to make peace, don't be discouraged. If you are the only one to suggest dates, quality time, or even sex, don't be discouraged. If you feel like you are the one holding your marriage together and you are at the point of breaking down from doing it alone, don't be discouraged. The Bible says, "And let us not be weary in well doing: for in due season we shall reap, if we faint not" (Gal. 6:9, KJV)

You may not see the change or the reward right away for everything you have sown. You might not even recognize it when it comes because it may not come in the form you wanted it to come. The fact is God cannot lie, and His word is true, you just have to have the faith to believe it. Drop your guns and sacrifice, compromise, love, forgive, and be a peacemaker. God will honor whatever you do to keep your marriage together. God will honor and bless you when He sees His character reflected in you. God will honor your faith in Him when He knows you are doing what you are doing out of obedience, and you don't even see any sign of change.

There are several reasons why people stick to their guns, but, as Christians, there is no reason to ever do so. Remember, the Bible says the battle is not yours but the Lord's. If your guns are pride, withholding money, withholding sex, withholding affection, or creating distance, put them down and trust God to do the rest. Either you are going to believe and follow what is in the word of God or not.

CHAPTER 12

The Button

If we live by the Spirit, let us also walk by the Spirit.
Let us not become conceited, provoking
one another, envying one another.
—Galatians 5:25–26, ESV

The Bible has made it clear that the spirit of the antichrist is already active in this world. The antichrist spirit promotes an agenda that either destroys or is the complete opposite of what God intended or created something to be. What does that mean for your marriage? That means that anything God has set into order, the enemy tries to destroy and come against it. The word of God says let no man separate what God has joined together. So naturally the enemy is going to do whatever he can to destroy marriage and God's design for a family. The Bible says, "So that we would not be outwitted by Satan; for we are not ignorant of his designs" (2 Cor. 2:11).

You need to understand the enemy does not want you to have a great marriage, nor does he want you to reach the point in your marriage where your marriage becomes a tool for the kingdom in the hand of God. Your marriage can help others through the power you give one another to accomplish what God has for you individually. There are things you can do individually, but at the end of the day, it's a team effort. What you accomplish together, and the testimony of your marriage is what can help other marriages overcome their problems as well. The enemy is going to do whatever he can to destroy this. Not only that but a marriage can produce children, and if both of you know who you are in Christ, and have a healthy relationship with Jesus, you can instill things in your children that will create a legacy of greatness that could affect generations. What you do affects more than just you and your spouse, but people around you, and the people around them.

You might never know how much of an impact you had until you get to heaven. You might be amazed by how many people you reached just by living a life that gave glory to God by never giving up when things got hard, and fighting through the hardest battles. You can have a much great impact than you think as an individual, and even more so as a couple and family. The enemy would love to do anything he can to destroy this union and all of your potential. He will do anything he can to cause a divide between you and your spouse. The Bible says a man who finds a wife obtains favor from the Lord, so of course, the enemy is coming for your favor and trying to destroy it. Don't be afraid of the enemy and expect the attack. Too many times people put the devil on the same level as God.

What you have to understand about the devil is he is not all-knowing nor is he all-seeing like God. The Bible says he is like a lion roaming the earth seeking who he can devour. He cannot read your mind. He cannot see in your heart. The only thing the enemy can see is what we do, what we say, and how we respond to things. Your spouse is usually the person you are the closest to. If he sees that every time you and your spouse argue, your relationship with God suffers, he is going to use that against you. If he sees every time you respond to something your spouse does in a sinful or angry manner, he is going to exploit that. If he sees when your spouse says or does certain things, and it opens your heart to temptations, he is going to exploit that. He is going to press that button over and over again if he sees it is effective in destroying your marriage, your motivation, your joy, and most of all, your relationship with God. Some people have marriage problems, and they get so consumed in fear and so depressed they become spiritually paralyzed. They find a corner to sulk in and their ministry stops, their worship stops, their Bible reading becomes obsolete, and this allows the enemy to have legal access to operate.

See, the enemy is just trying to find a way in. If he can get you to be sad, bitter, or angry, he can get his foot in the door. Once the enemy gets you in your emotions, he will offer up a compromise or temptation to lead you further into the trap. Have you ever noticed how every time your spouse says that one thing, it just sets you off? Maybe you get so angry you say a curse word or get physical. Maybe every time you and your spouse stop being sexual, you struggle with lust. The enemy sees that every time you and your spouse don't have sex for a period of time, the lust in you starts to rise up. So what he does is shoot the thought of porn, or he sends some temptation your way. Whatever it is, the enemy is always fishing for a response from you that he can hook you with, and take you down.

How do you overcome this? Many of us try to hammer down on our spouse and get them to stop being the problem. We say, "If you would stop doing this, we would stop doing that." In our minds, we look at the issue as action and reaction. We must realize that the Bible says we wrestle not against flesh and blood and that we are imperfect people in relationships with other imperfect people. We need to recognize when the enemy is trying to press our buttons and acknowledge what is really going on. Your spouse is not your enemy. The enemy is the devil. Are you going to continue to attack one another, or will you humble yourselves and exercise your God-given dominion against the enemy? Will you stand together and say despite what we are facing we come against this attack in the name of Jesus? Ask yourself is the enemy using me to press my spouses buttons? Is what I am mad about or attacking them about really that serious?

You have to take power of the thoughts in your mind, and control how you respond to adversity, disappointment, and failures inside of your marriage. When you stop letting the enemy get to you, he is going to have to find another way to get to you! The only reason you keep facing the same problem in your marriage is because you are not fighting against it in the right way. You must control your mood, your actions, and your reaction to others. No matter how unfair, no matter how bad the pain may feel, you must cast your cares to God and walk by faith and not by sight. Once the enemy sees that pressing that button is no longer effective and it is not influencing your praise, worship, faithfulness, or relationship with God, he will move on about his business and try to find another way to attack you. Your spouse is not your enemy. Sometimes, the enemy is just exploiting their unawareness to hinder and wound you. You must take control of yourself and fight everything the enemy throws at you with faith and the word of God. There is a right way and a wrong way to fight. The Bible says, "Casting down imaginations, and every high thing that exalteth itself against the knowledge of God, and bringing into captivity every thought to the obedience of Christ" (2 Cor. 10:5, KJV).

It is a waste of energy to try to bash, change, or even be angry with your spouse. The Bible says, "Blessed are the peacemakers." If you want to be blessed, be the peacemaker in your home, and let God fight your battles. If you realize that the enemy is exploiting you and using you against your spouse, take a stance against the enemy, and say never again. The enemy may be using the words you say, the way you react, or the lack of needs that you meet to take your spouse out. You must protect your marriage, your family, and the heart of your spouse from the poison of the enemy. If you see that something you do or say brings out the worse in your spouse, don't allow the enemy to use you as that button because you are in your feelings. Overcome your feelings and be a true Christian. Look at yourself and ask, "Would Jesus do this? Would Jesus be pleased with me causing confusion, division, hurt, and anger in my marriage?"

Like I said before, we are imperfect humans dealing with other imperfect humans, but we serve a perfect and all-knowing God. You may feel like your spouse is pressing your buttons looking for a reaction, so you want to press their buttons back, but remember, the Bible says, "Do unto others as you would have them do unto you!" Be the bigger person, and watch things change in your marriage quickly. Don't allow the enemy to run rampant in your marriage any longer!

This may require you to die to your flesh, your pride, your emotions, and everything your flesh is feeling to do in the moment, but this is how you know you are being a true follower of Jesus Christ. You must put your flesh on the cross for the greater good of your marriage. You should take no pleasure in seeing your spouse feel down or hurt. Refuse to press their buttons. Wake up and stop allowing yourself to be the button that is being pressed once you recognize it.

Since you are one, if you hurt your spouse, you are hurting yourself. If you wound your spouse, you are wounding yourself. You are only destroying your own marriage and hindering your blessings and your progress for your family by hurting your spouse. Many people don't understand that your wedding vows are a covenant between you, your spouse, and God. You are not only making a promise to your spouse, but making a promise to God. The Bible talks about how God despises vow breakers and how He hates divorce. It also says, "What God has joined together, let no man separate." The point is, don't get married if you are not ready to actually honor those vows. Honoring those vows means caring for one another, serving one another, loving one another through ups and downs, and protecting one another as well. You don't get in a marriage to destroy one another, you get into a marriage to multiply. Pressing each other's buttons only causes damage and gives the enemy access to hinder, tempt, and bring down your spouse.

The Bible says to give no place to the devil! God didn't give you a marriage so you can tear each other down. He gave you a marriage to make each other better for His glory. Stop wasting time fighting one another. Realize the enemy is exploiting you to distract you and hindering you from accomplishing and experiencing the purpose for your marriage. No person can complete you, but they can complement what God has already been doing in your life. Marriage has a purpose! You have to grow up and put away childish thinking and behavior. Marriage is not for kids. It is for grown people who have a purpose, direction, and the discipline to work through it.

Some people want the wedding and the benefits of marriage, but don't have the character to actually be what marriage requires of them. Imagine a baby playing with one of those games that has buttons and the buttons light up. The child sees the button light up, and they press it. When you see the button light up, you don't have to press it. You can save your marriage so much trouble and grief by not pressing the button. Your flesh will yell press it, hurt them the way they hurt you, win the argument, but the Spirit of God will say exercise the fruits of the Spirit. The devil wants to divide you, God wants you to come together and be fruitful.

> God blessed them and said to them, "Be fruitful and increase in number; fill the earth and subdue it. Rule over the fish in the sea and the birds in the sky and over every living creature that moves on the ground." (Gen. 1:28)

CHAPTER 13

Cheating Isn't Just Sex

For as he thinketh in his heart, so is he: Eat and drink,
saith he to thee; but his heart is not with thee.
—Proverbs 23:7, KJV

When people think of cheating in a marriage, their mind always goes to sex. The reality is that there is more ways that you can cheat in marriage other than sex. Not only can you cheat on your partner, but you can cheat them out of certain things as well. If you are spending all of your time on your phone and none of your time with your spouse that in itself is cheating your spouse. If they ask you to put away your phone and you find yourself getting upset or offended especially after being on it all day, you probably should slow down and realize that the attachment you have to your phone is not healthy for your marriage and that your partner probably isn't asking too much from you. If you are always hanging out with friends, going to the gym, focusing on work, and anything else that takes up all of your time, you are cheating your spouse out of something you should rightly be giving to them.

Of course, any of these things can eventually lead to the door of actually cheating physically, mentally or emotionally. When you spend all of your time in other places, the distance will grow between you and your spouse. It is easy to try to fill the gap with all of the temptation you can find on your phones through the internet and

118

social media. It is easy to find someone who shares common interests with you when you frequently go places you like, such as the gym. You have to remember the Bible says to give no place to the devil. By cheating your spouse out of quality time and companionship, you give the enemy something to use against you. If you are the one cheating your spouse out of time, you need to be wise and invest in your marriage. If you are the spouse getting cheated out of time, make sure you don't fall for the temptation the enemy will send your way to try to fill the void.

Tell God how you feel about what your spouse is doing and fill the void through worship, Bible reading, and spending time in the presence of God. Let God fight those battles for you. You not only one to close the doors to temptation for yourself, but by taking care of your spouse you assist with closing doors on some temptation for them as well. If you mistreat them, and do them wrong, and expect them to just take it and be a good Christian, that is unwise. You cannot put hope in any human being that they will just be strong and not fail. Better for you to just make the effort to do your part, as opposed to just doing whatever you feel and allowing the devil access into your marriage.

Not being honest is cheating your spouse out of intimacy because you can't have true intimacy in a marriage without honesty. You may not physically be engaged in cheating, but if you have to delete text messages or put a password on your phone because you don't want your spouse to see what you have been looking at online, that is cheating. When you drink from another well to quench your thirst that does not belong to you, you are cheating. This can be emotional, mental, or sexual. The Bible says that if a person entertains the thought in their mind, it is the same as if they actually did it.

When you have to lie, cover up, omit, or hide things, that is a relationship waiting to fall apart and be destroyed. The Bible says that what is done in darkness will always be brought to the light. The sad thing about it is that when the house starts falling apart, your selfish choices affect more people than just you. Your spouse, your kids, both sides of the family, and even future generations can be affected by you choosing to cheat, lie, and be absent in your marriage.

If you had an affair, you need to come clean and be honest about it. Give your spouse a chance to have the power to choose if they want to stay in the marriage. Affairs hurt either way, but the best thing you can do is be honest about it and give your partner the power to choose what they want to do. If you try to hide it and your partner finds out about it some other way, it will always be hard for them to trust you. If you choose to come clean yourself, the trust will grow back faster during the healing process.

If you are thinking about cheating, it may be best to sit your spouse down with someone you respect and come clean. Sometimes, by exposing the darkness and bringing it to the light, the temptation loses its power. Number one because the truth will set you free and because now you can have more people on your side praying against what is trying to destroy your marriage and holding you accountable. It is often when we live in darkness and keep things secret that sin is able to be birthed. Also, being honest with your spouse will more than likely anger them, but, at the same time, if they have gotten complacent in your marriage, it may give them the motivation to work harder at the marriage depending on what the reasons are for you entertaining having an affair. Some of you might say no way, but the reality is when people cheat, many spouses often end up asking why would you do this?

Sometimes, they are not surprised, and other times they are. It is possible that your spouse was unaware of how bad things really were, and if you had communicated with them, they may have made more of an effort. This is not saying it is okay to go and cheat if your spouse is failing in some area, but this is saying communication could of solved the problem in some cases as opposed to going out and cheating.

Some people may not agree, but that is why in our vows we say, "For better or for worse." You are choosing to love and be with someone through the ups and downs. You are choosing to make a commitment to somebody regardless of if they are the best version or worse version of themselves. At the end of the day, you have to come together through the good and bad and make a team effort to keep the enemy out of your marriage. If you enter a marriage, your mindset should be it is you and me no matter what, and getting a divorce is not an option. Many people don't go into marriage with that mindset anymore. If you really went into marriage thinking this was it, you would want it to be the best marriage it could be, and you would make more of an effort. Sadly, many people get into marriage and getting a divorce or entertaining other people depending on how good or bad the marriage is going is always an option. When they see that exit door always sitting there in their marriage, many people take the easy way out instead of fully committing to working it out.

I wouldn't go as far to say it is your fault if your spouse cheats on you because people cheat for many different reasons. There are people who have a close to perfect spouse who still cheat with random people they encounter. There are others who cheat because their spouse is not taking care of their needs at home whether emotional or sexual. Some people get mad when you ask them did they contribute to the cheating in anyway. In their mind, no matter how they treat you, what they failed to do or didn't do is in no way a reason to cheat. That is just simply immature, and not a very smart way of looking at marriage, let alone human beings. We all have needs, and when you enter a marriage, it is not an unrealistic expectation to think that your spouse is going to meet many of your needs. They can't meet all of them, only God can do that. But, the fact is as a wife you don't want another woman meeting your husband's needs, and as a man, you don't want another man meeting your wife's needs.

I would say that you need to be honest with yourself and ask could this door have been closed if you had or had not been doing something inside of your marriage. Far too many marriages get complacent, or they start thinking nobody else would want their spouse, so they stop making the effort. I ask you to daily consider what doors you are leaving open for your spouse to be attacked, consider their needs, and do your best to fill all the open spaces. There are some things that only God can do, but you have an obligation to your spouse as well. Many people don't like the sound of that word in marriage, but when you took vows, you made a commitment to your spouse, and you should do your best to honor it. God will honor your efforts and smile on your sacrifice.

CHAPTER 14

Loving Beyond the Hurt

But I say unto you, Love your enemies, bless them that
curse you, do good to them that hate you, and pray for
them which despitefully use you, and persecute you;
That ye may be the children of your Father which is in
heaven: for he maketh his sun to rise on the evil and on the
good, and sendeth rain on the just and on the unjust.
—Matthew 5:44–45, KJV

We live in an imperfect world with imperfect people. The reality is that you may come into this life like a blank piece of paper, but eventually you will get marked up. It is impossible to go through this life without getting hurt, lied to, taken advantage of, or having someone disappoint you. Some people have it much worse than others. People may have gone through so much heartache and pain in their lifetime that their hearts have become guarded and hard. They may have at one point in time been a very open, loving, and kind person, but because of what they have gone through, they have built up a wall of protection around their hearts.

How do you get beyond the hurt and revive what was once there or plant what never was? Some people have been hurt so badly that they are hard to love. These relationships can be very frustrating. You may often find yourself giving more than your spouse gives to you. This is not because your spouse is mean or that you are a better person, but you are just more open to give because your walls are down. People who have been hurt often try to protect themselves by putting up walls to keep people from getting too close. They have either been open with someone before who took advantage of them or they had someone take something from them without their permission like in cases of rape and molestation.

Often times, I have seen more women go through this than men, but I have seen plenty of men, as well as myself, who have been hurt as well. With most men, a man often fell in love with a woman, and that woman ended up cheating on them. Because of this wound, many men turn ice cold. They go around using females, but never opening up their heart to one ever again. Even if, by chance, a man does fall in love with someone and marries her, he will often have PTSD-like behavior in the marriage. Even if the girl that he is in a relationship with has never done anything to hurt him, he will find it hard to trust her and may find it hard to be open with her. This can be frustrating to a wife who is doing all of the right things. You are essentially paying for the damage someone else has done to your man's heart.

With females, it usually is a combination of things. Many men go around using, lying to, and breaking females' hearts. Sadly, many women give wife benefits to men who are not their husbands. They give so much of themselves only to see the men they have been pouring into one day leave, cheat, or even find out they are already married. Many women, like we mentioned before, have also had to endure the pains of dealing with molestation and rape. The other thing that can make many women hard is having to be the man. They get married and have kids and end up having to do all the things a man is supposed to do on top of being a mother. This could be because the man is just sorry, he has passed away, or he has exited the marriage.

God did not create woman to do a man's job, and He did not create man to do what woman can do. When you put the weight of being a man and a mother on a woman, they often become hard and ridged in a way that God never intended them to be. When men are tasked with doing what mothers do they usually make a mess, or do not do as good of a job, and even often try to find outside help too quickly. Of course, this is not true in all cases, but I have seen this come up several times.

The question remains—how do I break down the walls that my spouse has around in their heart? The first step is to realize that there is more than what you see at the surface. Don't get focused on the leaves that you see falling from the tree and dying. You need to find out what is the root of the problem. If you keep focusing on the leaves, you will end up in a cycle of always trying to rake up and clean season after season and never get to the real root problem. For instance, your spouse can have triggers that are causing them to behave or act a certain way toward you. Instead of taking this personally, you need to pray and communicate with your spouse and see what is truly behind their anger, depression, and rejection.

Maybe your spouse was called stupid their whole life by their parents and family members. You may see no problem with the word because you have used it as a joke your whole life, but when you say it to your spouse, the word brings back painful memories and insecurities. Because of the pain they feel, this causes them to put up a wall around their heart. This wall is built in order to protect them from disappointment and being taken advantage of. The wall can be built and have many different materials. The wall you may face is anger, and they use anger to mask the hurt they feel. The wall you could be starting as is distance. Because what you said hurt them or brought back bad memories, they distance themselves from you in order not to relive that pain. The wall you may be staring at could be rejection. Inwardly, they may not feel good about themselves or that they can meet your expectations or associate you with their past pain and, in return, reject your advances.

Many people look at a wall and they give up. Many people look at a wall, and they become bitter not realizing that the wall is not a sign that your spouse does not love you or does not care about you. It is simply a sign that they need help. If you always focus on the leaves and never get to the root of the problem, you will be counterproductive in everything you do to get beyond the wall to their heart. You may do something good in one area and you get your spouse to drop their guard, but when you touch that wound once more, it will cause them to put up another brick to replace the one you just removed. You have to learn how to approach the wall.

You must approach your spouse in the manner that God approached you. When Jesus hung on the cross, He was already very aware of all your failures, sins, and mistakes. He already knew that you wouldn't always do the right thing. At any point and time, He could have said, "I am going to come down. I am not going to hang on this cross for you any longer. I am not going to hang here because I know you won't stop sinning. I am not going to hang here because you'll take too long to repent. I am not going to hang here because I know you are going to backslide. I am not going to hang here because I know you will turn your back on me and walk away from the cross and embrace sin." Jesus hung on that cross with a love that goes beyond understanding. His love is patient, kind, and long suffering. He was willing to endure great pain for the greater good. He knew the only way to get the results that were needed was for him to endure. He didn't hang on the cross and be bitter. He didn't hang on the cross complaining and being condescending toward us. He never hung there thinking, *Look at you, you're such a mess. I can't believe I have to go through this for you.* When you realize how much Jesus loved you and how great His love is for you, it will make it easier for you to project that love toward your spouse.

The problem is that many people are selfish. Some people go through life always thinking about themselves and what is best for them. If you do this, it will be reflected in your actions and will also damage your relationships and cause you not to have patience for people. A selfish person will quit, be angry, or feel like it is a waste of their time if they are not getting something in return for their effort and time. This makes it impossible for a selfish person to serve and nearly impossible for a selfish person to have a good marriage. You have to take the focus off the small picture of how you feel and focus on the big picture of your marriage as a whole. If you focus on the fact that your needs are not being met, or that you are pulling more of the weight in the marriage, you will always be miserable and your relationship will end in destruction. A selfish person will look at their spouse and just be upset that they are not getting with the program. A selfish person will be upset that they have to do anything extra to make the marriage work. You will be mad at your spouse for being how they are without understanding why they are the way they are.

We mentioned before about being called stupid. If you realize that when you say something that triggers bad memories or a bad feeling in your spouse, you need to avoid that in order for them to heal. Don't expect them to just get over it. The way you take the wall down is by doing the opposite of what caused the damage. Encourage your spouse, and let them know that you think they are intelligent and smart and support those words with actions. Eventually, the insecurity will go away within your spouse, and some of that wall will be taken down. They won't be scared to share their ideas and thoughts with you because they will no longer worry about being rejected. You may also see a change in their behavior. See, they may seem to have an attitude or an angry countenance because of the frustration they feel inside. Even though they have built the wall, they may inwardly be waiting to get around or over it. They may have been wanting to share with you all of their thoughts and ideas, but couldn't overcome the fear of rejection or being called stupid again. Instead of explaining this to you, they act out in anger, depression, or distance. By removing some of the wall, you will see a change in their attitude as well.

Maybe you think your spouse is very needy. This can be very irritating and even unattractive to you depending on your personality. You just can't seem to understand why they are being so needy, and why they just can't be more like you. This goes back to being a selfish thinker. It is very possible that your spouse didn't get the love, attention, and affection they needed as a child. They may have grown up with a void inside of them and they are longing for someone to express love to them in that manner. It is not that they are needy; it may just be that they grew up with a handicap. Maybe you grew up in a home were you had all of those things, or you just have a personality where you are self-sufficient or not big on affection. When you belittle, reject, or make your spouse feel bad about coming to you for affection or being too needy you not only are putting up their wall, but also opening the door for temptation. A need is a need regardless of if you understand the need or respect it. The enemy will send someone else to take down the walls of your spouse, which will hurt them and, in turn, hurt you as well. All of this could be avoided just by finding the root of the problem and not getting offended and not give up when you see the leaves.

We talked earlier about people who have been molested and raped. Your spouse may reject your advances for sexual contact. They key here is to be patient and understanding. Many rape and molestation victims feel that their power to choose has been taken away from them. The first thing you can do to try to remove that wall is to be romantic. Try to put some effort into making it romantic and showing that you really love them and you are not using them for sex. The other is letting them be in control. Don't try to force, guilt, or pressure them into having sex with you. It is okay to make it be known because you have needs, but do it in patience and love. Let them come to you a few times. This empowers them with making the choice. They are choosing to engage in sex with you and not being forced or taken advantage of as in the cases of molestation and rape. This will paint a picture in your spouse's mind and show them that what happened to them in the past is not the same as the intimacy you have within your marriage.

I am not saying facing any of these things will be an easy task. It is going to require lots of patience, long suffering, and planting a lot of love. Whatever you want to see in your spouse, you must sow. If their hearts are hard, you must continue to sow gentleness and love. But, it is not enough to plant the seed. You must water it and protect it as well. What good is it to plant the seed one day, and come back the next and destroy it? Always remember how God was with you. Whenever you feel discouraged or you feel like giving up, think about what would have happened if God had given up on you.

I know it can be hard in these situations because many times you will feel like you are paying for someone else's mistakes. If you focus on what you are not getting in return, or the fact that you feel like you are doing all the work in your marriage, or all the suffering, you will never have the attitude it takes to get the wall taken completely down. The enemy will have you look at that wall and get offended, get discouraged, and depressed, but just remember your spouse is depending on you to help them. There is love, kindness, and a version of your spouse behind that wall that you have never seen just begging to get out and love all over you freely and uninhibited. The enemy will tell you it is not worth it, give up, but you must endure. Working on that wall will in turn allow God to work on you. In the end, both of you will actually come out better versions of yourselves and resemble more of what God had in mind for you before the walls ever started to go up.

The bottom line is that you are going to have to put your flesh on the cross. It may not seem fair, it may seem too hard, but, if you die daily to yourself every day, you will make progress and God will bless you for your labor of love. Don't believe the lies of the enemy and think it is hopeless. Even if it seems your spouse is not helping you at all to try to take down the wall keep the faith. After they see you being consistent, the wall will start to come down faster because every time you remove a brick and they don't get wounded their trust is being built. When their trust begins to build, they will be more willing to surrender and assist you in tearing down the walls that surround their heart. I leave you with this verse.

> Let us not become weary in doing good, for at
> the proper time we will reap a harvest if we do
> not give up. (Gal. 6:9)

CHAPTER 15

Our Marriage My Money

There is never a reason to fight about money. Money can
be made, but hurtful words can never be taken back.

I f you want to survive the for richer or poorer part of your vows,
there are a few things you need to understand about money in
marriage. Money is one of the biggest problems couples struggle
with in marriage. The way you avoid a lot of problems that many
couples run into is by being wise financially. Obviously, life has its
ups and downs, and sometimes, unexpected things happen;, but
many times, when couples are having issues with money, it could
have been avoided, or there is a wiser way to go about fixing it.

When you first start dating, money should definitely be something you guys talk about. I have always said what is the point of dating, if you are not thinking about potentially marrying the person?
You should be honest and upfront on both sides about income and
any debt that you may have. You should talk about spending habits,
savings plans, and get a feel for how one another handles money. You
should have the discussions at some point about if both of you would
work and what your long term plans are.

Many new couples just get hit with the love bug and they jump
into marriage and try to figure everything out as it comes. This is very
unwise and those unexpected variables that pop up in life can actually
cause you to look at your spouse in a different light. Some couples get

so caught up in their partner's looks, possessions, or whatever else it is and after they are married and life hits, they see the flaws. He is 6'2", but he is terrible with money. She is super beautiful, but she spends every dime she gets. He has a nice car, but his debt is through the roof!

Many people might not feel like they need to talk about "their money" with their potential spouse, but if you can't be honest and open now, what kind of marriage are you expecting to have? It is best to be upfront and honest so that you give the other person a fair chance to see what they are dealing with. This empowers them to make the choice to choose if this is something they want to roll up their sleeves and work on with you, as opposed to waking up feeling blindsided and trapped by something they knew nothing about.

We mentioned throughout this book that the Bible says the two flesh become one. This doesn't just mean spiritually. When you marry, everything that is yours becomes theirs. Your problems, your family, your possessions, and anything else goes from being "yours" to being "ours"!

The more honest you are with each other at the start, the better foundation you guys can build your marriage on financially from the start. Many people go into marriage like buying a fixer upper home. You got holes and bad plumbing you are trying to fix along the way, instead of just being patient, coming up with a plan and buying a newer home that needs no work.

You should have a plan financially before you get married. Obviously, getting married, you two will need money to put a roof over your head, food in the fridge, gas in the cars, and so forth. You should talk about how going from single life to married life will affect your transportation and your commute to work. You should talk about having children, or if you already have them what kind of financial obligation is there. When you get married, does your wife plan on quitting her job? Will you be able to sustain your standard of living you guys enjoy and meet the basic obligations of living? Will getting married right now be such a financially toll on you guys that you are struggling from paycheck to paycheck trying to make it, and you have no money for any type of recreational activities? What kind of savings do you guys have put away for a rainy day?

If you are getting married, hopefully, you trust the person you married. You guys should have a joint account and, if need be, separate accounts for yourselves and whatever you allow for yourself for spending and day to day living. If you feel like you can't trust your spouse with your half of the money, or access to your funds, you shouldn't be marrying that person. That is a huge red flag, and if you feel that way, you need to reevaluate getting married. You may feel that way because of something that happened in the past, or maybe just because you don't trust the person you are with. Either way, that is not a good way to start off a marriage.

If the husband is the only one working, you need to give your wife access to the funds. There are so many marriages where the wife does not work, but the husband is in control of all the money. Now, of course, if one of you is good with money, and the other one is bad, you have to work that out amongst yourselves as far as who is paying the bills and making the budget, but your wife should still have access. If you as the man are better with money, you need to set aside a part of your check that goes to her. She can have her own account with a direct deposit set up, or you can just give her money every time you get paid, but it is important that she has access to money. Too many men use money as a means of control in the marriage, and that is not Godly.

Ladies, if you are working as well, don't have the mindset that his money pays all the bills, and your money is just for you to spend on whatever you want. Any good man of course will pay the bills, but you being his helpmate should offer to help. If his paycheck is enough to cover all the bills, I suggest that your check goes toward building a savings account for the future.

Just because you have money, that doesn't mean you need to spend it. Some pay periods you should just sit around home in each other's company. Don't get so dependent on always having to spend money to have a good time in your marriage. Learn to just enjoy one another's company. Some couples are not happy if they are not spending money. What happens when you hit a rough season? What happens when the money is thin because of bills or children? Is your marriage going to collapse because the foundation of your happiness was spending money?

Don't get married for money, either. Don't marry a guy because he seems to be well off. You may love his money and his stability, but find out you don't love him. Even though you are rich in the bank, you are really poor in life. You will eventually become complacent and be frustrated trying to fill the voids in your life and heart that his money can't fill. Don't marry for opportunity or to be saved because you may be in a bad situation. Trust God, and wait for the right time. I have seen many women who are struggling because they are single mothers or other factors who marry a man for his money and end up being in a controlled situation, bitter, and very unhappy. Money can fix some problems, but it can't fill all voids.

The best marriages have lots of honesty and a plan based off that honesty. They look at each other's strengths and weaknesses and come together to build. If you approach your marriage by living out godly principles with your money and realizing that it is a team effort, you will save yourself a lot of stress.

When you are dating, you might talk about what you would name your kids, what kind of trips you would like to take, and many other things. Just make sure at some point in that process, when things get serious, that the conversation of money is put on the table, and you both are honest and open about it. This is wisdom, and you want to start off your marriage by laying the foundation with wisdom instead of leaving things to chance.

CHAPTER 16

How Do I Choose a Wife or Husband?

In all your ways acknowledge Him,
and He shall direct your paths.
—Proverbs 3:6, NKJV

You may have read this book and you are not even married. You may be asking yourself, *How do I choose the right wife?* Men, believe it or not, the wife you choose will be the biggest choice you ever make outside of following God. She will either help you build or tear down everything you do. She will either undermine your dream or expand your vision to go further than you even imagined you could. She will either hold you up when you are down or kick you and tell you to stop being weak. She will either be a good mother to your children or a bad one. She will either have your trust through her actions or she won't. She will either guard your heart or break it. She will either bring out more of what God put in you or beat it down into a corner. The Bible speaks of two types of women. At the end of the day, in every passage about women, they either build or destroy something. Will she build or destroy your ministry, dream, heart, drive, and your resources? There is so much more to choosing a wife than, "Look at her. She is fine!"

You need to realize the investment, work, and time you will be putting in to build with her. You need to choose with more than your eyes and lust being the determining factors of whether she is a good choice and investment into your life. The word of God gives you the outline and relationship with God ordering your steps. Let God choose for you. If you choose wrong, you will end up in a world of hurt, and often can bring kids into a situation that causes them to grow up with a handicap. Kids benefit from having a family structure the way God intended for the family to be, but if you choose wrong, you will build wrong, and things can fall apart. If the children grown up with that handicap, they can become adults and make the same mistake. Understand that your choices can not be selfish, and they must be based on wisdom and the principles found in God's word in order to succeed.

We have established the qualities of what makes a godly man or godly woman. We have established what God requires of you individually and both of you collectively. When you are looking at a woman that you are thinking about pursuing, the first thing you need to do is pray about it. Sometimes, God will just simply tell you no right from the start. God won't even allow you to waste your time. The problem is we often don't have the clearest connection with God when it comes to what we want. We often hear those other voices getting mixed in with the voice of God. If you find yourself not being able to tell the difference between God's voice and yours, get someone to join with you in prayer. I always suggest going to your pastor, especially if you are interested in someone who attends the same church as you. I think it should be clear that looking to marry someone outside of your faith is a no go. The Bible says, "Do not be yoked together with unbelievers. For what do righteousness and wickedness have in common? Or what fellowship can light have with darkness?" (2 Cor. 6:14, NIV).

That scripture lets you know that if you choose to get involved with someone, you better win them to the faith before even considering marrying them or being in any kind of relationship. There is a verse that says the unbelieving spouse can be saved through a saved spouse, but that does not mean go out and marry someone who is not saved. That verse was written knowing that some people would already be married before they came to Christ.

When you get married, you guys become one in God's eyes. Your marriage should bring glory to God, so in order for the marriage to give Him the most glory, you should strive to help each other become the best version of yourself. This goes back to how we opened this chapter. You want your wife to help you with your walk with God and not be a hindrance. You want her to help push you closer to God and not influence you to go further away. No matter how kind she might be, if she does not share your faith, you will be unequally yoked. If you are really interested in her have prayed about it, and you feel God is telling you she is the one, you must do your best to win her over. Invite her to church, get her connected with some sisters in your church, and maybe even do a few Bible studies with her. I have come to find out that when a woman really loves and trusts you, she will be willing to follow where you lead her.

This is a place where many believers mess up. They start dating or having kids with people outside the faith, and after they are so deeply committed, they try to fix the problem with marriage. Instead of pulling them into the church, you've gotten pulled into sin. How many times have you seen a church girl start talking to some guy in the world end up pregnant and leaving the church? How many times have you seen some guy marry a girl outside the faith and end up miserable? The Bible says, "How can two walk together unless they agree?" Somebody is eventually going to get pulled in the other direction if you both are not walking in the same direction.

If you look at the story of Samson, he tried to live for God, and do the things that God had asked him, but because he got involved with the wrong woman, the blessing and ministry God had given him was destroyed. Are you willing to sacrifice or put in danger everything God has for you because you are not thinking with a clear head? Even though both partners need to be praying, and both partners need to focus on helping one another, I put the attention on the man first because the Bible says when a man finds a wife, he finds a good thing. So it really starts with the man, and hopefully the woman is in tune with God to know that not every man who steps to her, is sent from God, even if it does look like a good fit.

The truth is that many people in this world we are living in have had sex with their partner before they married them. Sex clouds judgment, especially for men. Even if you are not actually sinning and having sex before marriage, just entertaining the thought of having sex with a person can consume you. You lose your focus when you are drawn away and led by your lust. You are not able to focus on the right questions that are outlined for you in the word of God. People mistake lust for love all the time. Sometimes, all the sex block out all the other things. You never noticed they were not clean, had a bad attitude, or had past wounds they never healed from because all you focused on was the sex and their body.

Are you pursuing her, or allowing him in because you are lonely? Do you think she/he is the only one who is interested in you? Do you desire her/him sexually and are blind to everything else? Do you think you need to get married because you guys got pregnant? Are you thinking you guys are a good match because of your outward appearance together? If these are at the forefront of your mind, you have a very good chance of stepping into a bad situation and being destroyed. If all you think about is her looks, you are not able to ask yourself is she a Proverbs 31 type of woman? Does she have a healthy relationship with God? Is she faithful to God? If she is not faithful to God, she may not be faithful to you. If she does not have a healthy relationship with God, her relationship with you could waver when things get hard. If she is not a Proverbs 31 woman, rest assured she is going to make your life hard. Is it worth it? Is fulfilling your lust or being impatient worth it?

Young men need to realize that getting married is a tremendous responsibility. It is more than just getting married to have sex, have someone to cook for you, keep you company, and have babies. That woman you marry has her own mind, desires, and relationship with God. When you choose to marry her, you are choosing to marry everything she comes with. If you are not paying attention, you will wake up surrounded in a big mess. Is she compatible with the direction God is taking your life? Does she desire to go in that direction and support your dream? Do your dreams match up? When you marry a woman and you lay with her, you become one with her. Depending on who it is, you are either going to have two good halves come together and make one awesome whole marriage. Or, you will have two opposites come together that will strain, pull away, and destroy one another. You must seek God in every step you make. You must allow God to choose the wife that is best for you. You may think that you know what you like, but God knows what you need. Let Him guide you to the special woman He has for you.

Ladies, there is not going to be much here for you in this chapter. We mentioned before that God says, "A man who finds a wife finds a good thing." You have the power to choose who you entertain, who you give your time to, and ultimately who you say yes to. If you want to be safe, ask yourself is this man lining up with what the Bible says a man should be before you date him? Is this man faithful to the church? Does this man submit to Godly leadership in his life? Does this man love his mother and family? Even if you think the answer to all of those questions is the right one, the next step is to pray and include your parents.

This may sound old school, but if you have a father in your life, the guy who wants to date you should have no problem meeting your father if he has good intentions. If your father is not in your life, go to your pastor. I say this because before you even open the door and get too emotionally connected, you should allow an older man to have a chance to kind of read the guy you are interested in. Just like men can make silly judgment because they get all googly eyed for a females looks, ladies can do the same for a man who knows how to talk a good game. The Bible says, "There is safety in a multitude of counseling." I would suggest that you get your pastor and your parents involved at least with the initial meeting. If you are not dating to get married, then what is the point? Don't waste time even getting involved with someone just because you are bored, lonely, or because they just happened to be there and be available. Let God be at the very center of the start of that relationship, and He will be there all the way to the end.

CHAPTER 17

It's Just Not Working

> ²⁸ And we know that all things work together for
> good to them that love God, to them who are
> the called according to his purpose.
> — Romans 8:28, KJV

What do you do when it looks like your marriage is falling apart despite all of your efforts? What do you do when you feel like the harder you try to keep things together, the greater the distance becomes between you and your spouse? You may have read all of these chapters and said. "I have done that, tried that, and things just keep getting worse." It is very hard not to be bitter, to quit, or to even resist temptation in times like this. In the world we are living in, the easy thing to do is just throw in the towel and call it quits. I always ask people though, did you commit to your marriage like there were no other options? Because when people are married, but they entertain the thought of being with somebody else, or being in a better situation, they will always exit. But, if you go into marriage thinking, no matter what it is you and me, people tend to make more of an effort to make it work. If you feel you have done all you can do, counseling, prayer, and made the effort, it is possible that sometimes it just won't work, and it could be for many reasons. What do you do when it just doesn't work?

I have been there before. Sometimes, after you have done everything you can, you just have to stand still and let God take full control of the situation. You may just have to embrace the distance and draw closer to God. I do believe that at any time God could prick a person's heart and change them around, but the reality is what we want and what God wants does not always match up. What's even harder to understand is that many times, He is trying to work something through us by using what we are going through. You can compare it to cooking something on the stove. If you don't cook it long enough, it won't be suitable to eat, and if you cook it too long it will burn.

God is a master chef when you look at it from this aspect. He knows just how long to keep you in a situation to work what He is trying to work in you. The thing is to not look at your spouse or ex as the enemy. Legalistic people will tell you things like God hates divorce, and if you get divorced, you failed, and there must be something wrong with your spiritually, but this is simply not true. Like I said before, people always get involved in things that God never had planned for their life, and He allows it because of our free will. What you need to remember is that the Bible says all things would work for our good, so don't get all distraught about whatever you are facing. Walk by faith and not by sight even in the ugliest of situations.

The problem is we often get so panicky that we focus on our fears, insecurities, and hurts, and forget all about divine purpose. I have told many husbands and wives in difficult situations that sometimes God will allow your spouse to keep on behaving in the manner they are until you get your focus right. For some of us, God has to allow the thorn to be in our side because that is the only thing keeping us saved. If your marriage was going smoothly, you wouldn't pray anymore. If your spouse was acting perfectly, you would get comfortable and lose your drive for seeking God. It may not seem like things are working because what God is working on you, you may not even recognize.

You want God to work on your spouse, but He is working on you. If you would be patient and let God work on you, you may find out things will change quickly in your marriage as well. Many people often have too much pride to even admit that they could be part of the problem in the marriage, but God knows best. God can also be allowing your spouse and you to go through it because you have made them or your relationship an idol and have put it above the Lord. When your idol fails you, you run back to God, and that is what He wanted in the first place. Not to make your relationship bad, but for Him to be at the center of it.

The first thing you should do if your marriage is not turning around is fall on your face humbly before God and ask if there is anything that you are or aren't doing that is preventing change. You need to ask God if there is anything that He is trying to work on you to make you a better Christian through what you are going through? If you seek God, and there is something there, He will identify it to you. The reality is that it might not always feel good to accept what God is showing you. You may come to find out that you are the biggest problem in your marriage or that your spouse was actually right about something. Many marriages don't make it simply because of this pride. Our first instinct is to just blame the other person instead of looking in the mirror. God will deal with you before He deals with your spouse, even more so when you are the head.

You have to be able to crucify your pride and say, "Lord, I put this battle in your hands." You have to be able to crucify your pride and ask, "Lord, is there anything I am doing wrong?" You have to crucify your pride and be willing to take the focus off of your spouse and all their imperfections and focus on yourself. You have to crucify your pride and acknowledge and accept if God reveals something to you that you didn't know about yourself. You may have to pray for God to give you the grace and strength to change what needs to change or endure a situation that is unpleasant. When you don't know what else to pray or do, pray for God's will to be done in your life, and your marriage.

Sometimes, we can be proud and think we are the sole reason our marriage is working or still together. God will sometimes allow us to be humbled by changing the circumstances of our marriage. He may even allow things to get so bad that you have no choice but to acknowledge that without Him, your marriage would be over and beyond hope. Some spouses will even look down on their spouses and become condescending. "If it wasn't for me, this marriage would have been lost a long time ago."

"I am holding this together, you don't do anything to contribute to this marriage." Saying things like that often cause more damage and resistance than good. You make it seem like the person is lucky to be with you, or that you are doing them a favor by being with them. Instead of being there because you love them, you look at them as like a charity case, and you are just so generous to be putting up with them. Walking in this kind of arrogance is never good for your marriage, it is always better to walk in humility.

You have to understand that your marriage is not all about you and that God cares for your spouse as well. So, even if you are doing no wrong in your own eyes, God may see wrong that you are doing toward your spouse from His perspective. Because He loves your spouse just as much as He loves you. He will put His hand in the middle of the situation. You must also remember that everybody often thinks they are right. Some people are so caught up in being right that they can become blinded to the fact that they are completely wrong even when presented with evidence. I honestly don't know why humans are like that, but I have even been that way sometimes. God will help open our eyes to ugly truths about ourselves.

You and your spouse may both be praying to God about each other with the mindset that the other one is the problem, but God is able to see what is really going on. You may see some things about your spouse that they can't see, but, at the same time, they may see some things about you that you don't see. At the end of the day, God has a perspective where He can see it all.

That is why when you pray to God and you go to Him with concerns, you must go to Him empty. Some of us are so full of ourselves, our feelings, and our thoughts that there is no room for anything or anyone else. We are so full of pride that we can't even receive the idea that we might be wrong or the one with issues. We go to God so full that there is no room for Him to put anything in us. When you pray for your marriage, you keep praying for God to change your spouse, but never ask the Lord to search your heart and expose anything that you may be doing wrong to you. This is why God allows us to struggle and be in situations where we become desperate for Him. If we are not willing to die to our flesh on our own, God will aid us in our flesh being made uncomfortable.

People often ignore the urgings of the Spirit to follow the desires of their flesh. Your Spirit may lead you to forgive, submit, love, or be humble, and your flesh will create distance, be mean, get revenge, or ignore them. When you give into what your flesh wants over and over again, you become carnally fat and spiritually skinny. This imbalance in you will affect your marriage, and, if you cannot identify it on your own, God will put you in a place that will allow you to see yourself. The fact is just because you feel like God's word and system is not working does not mean that it isn't.

The sad reality is that sometimes marriages do come to an end. People fall out of love, and no matter what, it takes two to tango. The hard part to recover a marriage is when both partners fall out of love. Often, marriages that make it, make it because both partners never fell out of love at the same time. You always had somebody fighting on behalf of the marriage. There can come a point that no matter what you do, it is out of your hands. You may feel like you have tried everything and gave it literally everything you have, but it just wasn't good enough. In these moments before you do anything rash or follow your emotions, just sit back and wait in the presence of God. If it comes to an end, allow God to have full control of that situation. Just stand still on the word of God, and let whatever unfolds unfold and no matter what the end result, rejoice because you know all things will work together for the good of them that love Him and are called according to his purpose.

CHAPTER 18

The Transition From Hurting To Healing

Healing one day is always one day at a time.

It would be nice if all marriages and relationships worked out. It would be nice if all of us could connect with the right person the first time, and nobody ever got their heart broke, cheated on, abandoned, or divorced. Unfortunately, this is just not how it always works. Many relationships end badly because people don't build with the proper foundations we talked about in previous chapters. People get into relationships for the wrong reasons and without really knowing themselves. Instead of growing together, the two people grow apart as they begin to learn things about themselves. I didn't even know what I liked and didn't like at the age of nineteen. I didn't know who I was as a man or what God was calling me to do. It made no sense for me to get into a marriage.

We kind of learned things about ourselves along the way, and it just didn't mesh well. This is unfortunate, but I always say every good idea isn't a God idea, and just because someone is good to you, doesn't mean they are the one for you. My ex-wife is a wonderful, kind person, but we just were not meant to be together. We didn't pray about it, we didn't fast about it, we just followed our feelings. We tried to build something on the foundation of feelings instead of principles, and so when everything collapsed, it was not really a surprise. The worse part about it is that during the collapse people get wounded by all the falling pieces.

Then, of course, there are people out there who use other people, and never had intentions on changing negative behavior or making the effort to make it work. Some people just play a role long enough to get whatever they can out of the relationship. Some people are looking for sex, money, saving from bad situations, companionship because they are lonely, or just a rebound to help them get over a recent breakup. They can lead a person on into thinking they actually wanted the relationship to grow into something more, and this is very unfortunate for the person who falls for it, and actually makes an emotional investment in the relationship.

It can be devastating to realize you put so much effort into something that failed, or that you were in it all alone the whole time. It can make you feel less than, rejected, broken, and leave you with serious trust issues. The wounds can be so great that your fear of ever committing or getting into another relationship will paralyze you and keep you from ever moving forward with your life. You can't change the fact that you got hurt, but you can control how long you allow it to keep you down. Some people make the mistake of being in denial and trying to act like they are not hurting, and this just prolongs the healing process because they never address the bleeding wound. There is absolutely nothing wrong with admitting you are hurt and taking time to hurt, but eventually, that hurt needs to transition into healing. Don't allow the hurt to keep you from allowing people in your life who want to help you and love you. Don't allow the hurt in your life to determine what your self-worth is. Don't allow the hurt in your life to cause you to settle for something less than what you deserve.

Everybody heals differently, and if you are dealing with somebody who is hurting, don't get mad at them for hurting, be patient. Don't belittle or try to downplay how they feel because they are not you. The truth is you may get into a relationship and the person might not even know they were still hurting but being in a new relationship brings up some of those old wounds. Nevertheless, don't get frustrated with how they react to what they have been through.

Maybe you wouldn't respond to what they went through the same way, but the reality is, you are not them, so all you can do is love, be patient, and pray for them.

If you are the person trying to heal, make sure you focus on the positive and not the negative. Make sure you allow your mind to be saturated in the love and word of God. The biggest thing that will keep you from healing is how you think about what you have been through and surrounding yourself with negative and bitter people. If you don't bring your thinking under control, you will prolong the healing process and prevent yourself from moving forward and experiencing everything God has for you. I know it hurts, I know you invested a lot, I know it doesn't feel good to be cheated on, rejected, or even for you to be the one who messed up, and realize you can't go back and change what you did after you lose everything. The reality is though, that what's done is done, so how can you move forward with your life?

The first thing God showed me when I went through some of the ugliest parts of relationships was that the Bible says all things work together for the good of them that love Him and are called according to His purpose. I remember I was crying, broken, and depressed, but the words all things kept echoing in my head. Not somethings, not somedays, not sometimes, but all things all the time. That means that the break up, the cheating, the lying, the heartbreak, and even my failures will all work for my good if I continue to trust God. Somehow, someway, God is going to turn it around for my good. I have to trust God even when I can't trace Him. I have to praise Him for the doors He opens, as well as the doors He shuts. Maybe that door just wasn't meant for me. Even though it seemed right to me, and even though I felt like I couldn't live without it, God knew something that I didn't know, He saw something I couldn't see; and because of His love for me, He closed that door despite my efforts to walk through it. This is real faith! Trusting God even when you don't like it or when you don't get what you want.

Remember God's ways are not our ways, His thoughts are not our thoughts. Just because it made sense to you, does not mean it lined up with God's will for your life. You need to trust the fact that what God has for you is better than what walked out of your life or hurt you. If you can't trust God like that, you will never experience the amazing things He has for you because you will be too busy playing god over your own life and making a mess of things trying to be in control. The children of Israel took forever to go into the promise land because they kept messing with idols and doing their own thing instead of trusting God. Some of the relationships you enter, you made those people idols. Stop letting an idol have power over you and move forward in Jesus name.

This is not the end for you. Yes, they left you. Yes, you may have made a bad choice that messed up your marriage. Yes, they cheated on you. Yes, you are lonely, but this is not the end. There is nothing too broken that God cannot restore and fix. The question is, what is God's will for your life? Forgiveness does not always mean reentry and seeking someone's forgiveness does not always guarantee they will take you back. God wants you to forgive, let go, and accept forgiveness and be free from condemnation. Either He will restore it or He will replace it, either way, you must trust Him through the hurt.

God is not going to leave your or forsake you, He is very aware of what you have went through. His eyes were on you the whole time, the question is how will you respond? When you can stand under the weight of the pain, that is true faith. When you can lift your hands and worship despite the wounds, that is true faith. God allowed the test to happen to see how you would respond. God will use these trials to make you stronger than ever. He will use the pain for a testimony in your life that will give Him glory. Don't allow your relationship with God be determined by what you are going through with other people. Be faithful to God, and He will be faithful to you. He will comfort you, strengthen you, and bless you if you keep pressing forward.

Before you transition into a new relationship after coming out of a bad one, there are many things you should consider. Are you healed to the point that you will not allow your past wounds to bleed all over your new relationship? Will you be able to trust and love this new person without holding what someone else did to you against them? Are you still in love with the person you broke up with? You don't want to still be in love with the person from your past because you will not dedicate yourself fully to the new relationship. The first step to healing is honesty. Don't lie to yourself about what you are really feeling and the role you played in whatever occurred.

The pain gets worse if you were the one who was rejected in the relationship, because that could leave a desire in you to chase their acceptance. This can lead to a very unhealthy pattern of living. Every time they snap their fingers you drop everything and keep running back to them. They don't change, but because you want to be accepted and loved by them so bad, you keep dropping everything and running back. Stop dropping everything to run back to someone who did you wrong. Lose the desire to have their acceptance and love and get over the rejection.

Many people will run back to a bad relationship because they want to be accepted and not rejected. You are not running back to them because you love them, you are running back to them because when they rejected you, it gave them power over you. It made you feel bad to be rejected, it hurt your self-esteem. You didn't like how they treated you, you didn't love being disrespected, but you find yourself running back when they call because you have not healed from the wound they inflicted on you. If you stay in this pattern of dropping everything every time they call, you will mess around and drop a good thing chasing after a bad thing. Don't miss your blessing chasing a blunder. You will never heal running back to the person who inflicted the wound and they didn't change. I don't believe in closure, I believe in the power of Jesus Christ that can heal and mend a broken heart. So, before you jump into a new relationship, ask yourself have you broken free from the old one?

You want to be able to be honest in a relationship. If you cannot be honest, you cannot have true intimacy. Are you able to be vulnerable with the person you are seeing, or do you find yourself putting up walls? Many times, we put up walls because we feel that if we showed the person the real us, they would reject us. This is not a good way to start a relationship, and this is also a form of manipulation and deception. You shouldn't manipulate your way into someone's life. If you are serious about being with them, you need to be able to be honest with them and allow them to decide if they want to pursue the relationship. It is unwise to hide things only for them to be revealed later on, and that person feel betrayed, or forced into dealing with something they never even had the option of choosing if they wanted to deal with it. If you can't trust the person you are with to love you regardless, maybe that is not the one you need to be taking vows with saying for better or for worse, because you never allowed them to see the worse.

You want to go into a relationship being honest, being transparent, and being true to who you are. Of course, during the relationship, you might have to adjust somethings in order for it to work, but when you initially go in, you want to be honest with who you are as a person, and what you have been through. I am not saying you have to tell every little failure and ugly detail of your life, but the things that affected you or hurt you deeply should eventually be discussed and put on the table for entering a marriage. If you can't freely talk about it without getting to emotional, that might be a sign that you have not healed yet.

Before you transition into a new relationship, make sure that you are not transitioning with any bags that you don't need to take with you to your new destination. You don't need bitterness, unforgiveness, resentment, fear, and things that could be toxic in your new relationship. Remember, in a marriage, the man and woman become one, so whatever you bring with you, will become one with your relationship no matter how much you try to hide it or suppress it. Don't suppress it, address it, and allow God to complete whatever work needs to be done inside of you. Some people lie to themselves and because of pride try to act like what they went through didn't hurt them. Remove your pride and release all of the pain and hurt. If you have to cry, cry and give it to God. Once you leave it all at the altar, get up and don't pick it up anymore. Don't worry about it, don't meditate on it, don't go back and message that person, don't revisit those old wounds, just release it to God, and move forward with your life in Jesus name.

Sometimes, in order to move on, you have to allow the brokenness to come. Allow yourself to be broken in the presence of God, get it all out of your system, and be vulnerable before the Lord. Let Him know how you feel, let Him know what you fear, and ask Him to do whatever needs to be done in you for you to move forward with your life.

When you get ready to try a relationship again just remember, when you get hit, attacked, and wounded you go into a defensive posture. Don't allow how the last person who hit you cause you to always be in a defensive posture looking to get hit. Just because the last person wasn't loyal, doesn't mean the next one won't be. Just because the last person played games, doesn't mean the next one will to. Just because the last person broke your heart, doesn't mean this one will also. I know you got accustomed to getting hit, but don't go into that new relationship always looking for the hit. When you cover up looking for a hit, you are not open up to fully receiving the love they have for you. Let your guard down, ask God to order your steps, and use wisdom.

CHAPTER 19

Are You in Real Love?

Do you really know what love is?

What is love? It seems that the world does not truly understand what love really is. Love is more than an emotion or a warm fuzzy feeling in your stomach. Love is not always going to feel good. There are going to be times where you are just simply not feeling the love. There are going to be times where it actually hurts you to love. There are going to be times where you will have to press through in order to love. There is going to be a time where your love is tested and you will feel like failing. True love does not mean you will never run into problems. True love means that despite the problems, the love won't change.

Love is not a noun, it is a verb. Love is not something you just say or feel; it is something that you do. We live in a world where people say, "I love you," all the time and don't really mean it. Many times, what they say is not adding up with what they do. When you choose to marry someone, you are making a commitment to love them through the good and the bad. You are making a vow to love the beautiful and not-so-beautiful parts of who they are. True love is not conditional. True love does not make threats or manipulate. True love says, "It is you and me through it all until the end no matter what or who comes and goes."

The fact is that your partner will eventually do something you don't like or agree with, but, if you really love them, that shouldn't make the feeling fade away. The Bible talks about how love endures and is patient. Is your love willing to endure? Is your love willing to take a stand against everything that is going to come against your marriage and try to destroy what God has put together? Are you going to fight for what you signed up for, or simply throw in the towel and quit? Can you look in the mirror and say, "I truly have my partner's best interest at heart, even above my own?" Love is not selfish. Love is not narcissistic. Love gives more than it takes.

I believe you shouldn't have to dig and beg for the love of the one you are with, but granted some people are hurt. Sometimes, you will have to love them through certain seasons of their lives, but that's just what it should be, a season. Some seasons, you are going to do more sowing than you will reaping, but eventually, you should see the fruit and return of all your love and effort. Just know as you sow, that we are all imperfect people serving a perfect God who is perfect love, and the way He loves we should emulate in our day to day lives no matter what the current conditions are.

If you are making a lifetime commitment to somebody, you should want them to have the best life ever. Don't marry to nag them and fight all of the time, or to even control them. Don't keep your partner back from being everything they are called to be. Love wants your partner to be the best version of themselves that they can be. Love will stand by their partner and push them, and support them to go up to that next level. Love will say, "What do you need from me to be a success? I want you to have the best life you can possibly have, and I am here to help in any way I can." If you wake up thinking how to tear down your spouse or how to control or manipulate them into doing things your way, that is not love. If you are always trying to bully your spouse so you can have everything revolve around you, that is not love. Love is compromise and coming to a middle ground when you disagree or don't feel like doing somethings that marriage requires.

Maybe you feel like you are married, and the love is not there. The amazing thing about love is it can be planted, watered, and protected, and it will grow. You can start doing things to make your spouse fall in love with you more. You can start doing things to make yourself more loveable, but, in order to do so, you must be selfless. Just because you are not feeling the magic one day, does not mean it is time to throw in the towel. If you don't feel the love, grow the love.

If you are really in love with someone, there should be evidence in your actions. They should be able to look at the way you live your life and say, "Yes, my spouse loves me." Sometimes, there are people who are insecure and you just have to work with it. But, before you slam them and say they are insecure, ask yourself if there are things that you are not doing or could be doing to make them feel insecure. If you gave me your baby, and I started recklessly throwing her around in the air, you wouldn't feel very secure, and you probably wouldn't let me hold your child anymore. If I give you my heart and my love, and you start abusing it recklessly, it will probably be hard for me to trust you again.

When you wake up every day of your marriage, remember that love is more than words you say with your mouth. It is an action that needs to be lived out over and over again. It is a lifetime vow that you made or are planning to make between your spouse and God. That is very serious. God cares about the way you carry yourself in your marriage and the way you treat your spouse. Remember, God is love, and we are supposed to be a reflection of who He is.

> Love is patient, love is kind. It does not envy, it does not boast, it is not proud. It does not dishonor others, it is not self-seeking, it is not easily angered, it keeps no record of wrongs. Love does not delight in evil but rejoices with the truth. It always protects, always trusts, always hopes, always perseveres. (1 Cor. 13:4–7, NIV)

CHAPTER 20

The System Works

It's good if god created it.

What I want people to understand is that God's system works. People often think Christianity or religion is just not working for them, when the fact is that they are just doing something wrong, or they missed a step. Somewhere along the way, they took a shortcut or have a negative perspective because they are not properly equipped with what they need to make it through. Other times, we simply had a bad example or had someone teach us the wrong way. Now, because that is all we know, we have become loyal to dysfunction. Many marriages could be saved and blessed if we started really seeking God and being honest with ourselves. Pride always comes before a fall. Being lazy is a recipe for destruction and being complacent always allows the enemy to sneak in. If most people were honest with themselves about a failing relationship, they could look back and see where it went wrong. Maybe they didn't ask God if it was okay to date this person and they just followed their feelings. Maybe they didn't wait for marriage and were having premarital sex. Maybe things started good, but somewhere along the road, they got in their feelings and did the opposite of what God told them. At some point, they followed their feelings instead of the blueprint in God's word.

Everything we need is made available to us, but many people don't take the time or make the sacrifice that is necessary to learn the steps that need to be taken in order to have a blessed and victorious life. Many people resort to having a this-is-just-the-way-I-am attitude, and you can take it or leave it. God is not pleased with this kind of thinking because through His power and Spirit living in us, we should be overcomers and portray His characteristics in our marriages. We have the power to be transformed, we don't have to stay the same way year after year. God has given us His Spirit, and through His Spirit, we can overcome the carnal man that fights against lining up with God's will for our life and marriage.

The Bible says to let no man separate what God has joined together, but the fact is that most of us are putting our own pieces together and leaving God completely out of the equation. We try to model off of someone else's marriage, television, or follow what our parents did or failed to do, when this is not the direction God has for us. God deals with everyone uniquely. His word applies to everybody just the same, but we all have different personalities, gifts, strengths, and weaknesses. Maybe what your mother taught you would work isn't working in your marriage because your husband is nothing like your father. Maybe what you expect of your wife is not happening because you're expecting her to be like your mother. Many times, you are simply miserable because instead of looking at your marriage as something fresh and brand new to build, you are taking too many parts from other people and trying to implement them into your unique marriage from God. Instead of finding the unique beauty inside of your marriage, you are trying to reflect someone else's. In order to find the beauty in your marriage you will have to dig for it. It might be some work, and require some sweat, but you will find that diamond if you keep looking!

Many people look at other couples and wonder why their marriage is better or their life seems more blessed. The reality is that God's word works the same for everybody if we follow it. We have to focus on our God-given role. It is not enough to just follow it because we think that is what God wants. We must embrace it with the right heart and give it all we have. When you follow something just because you feel it is a rule, you will grow to resent it. When you actually have faith and trust God, and buy into His blueprint for marriage, you will see it is easier to be excited about doing your part. You realize that if you do your part, God will take care of the rest. I always like to say, fall in love with Jesus, and everything else will fall into place. When you fall in love with Him and His word, it will open doors for you that you didn't even know where there. Embrace everything that Jesus has for you. Trust him when you can't even trace Him.

We live in a world where everyone is trying to defy what God created them to be. There are men who want to be women and women who want to be men. There are husbands who want to do what wives do and wives who want to do what husbands do. Often times, we focus way too much on the other person's role that we neglect our own. We think that we know how to do what God has asked of them better than they do. We spend so much time looking at their flaws that we are blind to our own.

> And why beholdest thou the mote that is in thy brother's eye, but considerest not the beam that is in thine own eye?
>
> Or how wilt thou say to thy brother, Let me pull out the mote out of thine eye; and, behold, a beam is in thine own eye?
>
> Thou hypocrite, first cast out the beam out of thine own eye; and then shalt thou see clearly to cast out the mote out of thy brother's eye. (Matt. 7:3–5, KJV)

If we spent just as much time focusing on what God asks of us, our marriages would be better. The thing is that people don't really believe what the Bible says. If we really trusted God's word, we wouldn't be distracted by what everyone else was or was not doing. We need to have the mindset of "I know if I do what God asks of me, He will take care of the rest. He will either convict or change my spouse, give me the strength to endure, or remove them from the equation." The truth is that many people don't like doing right and not seeing a return. What we fail to realize is that sometimes, we are seeing a return, but it is not coming in the way we thought it would. Maybe the fact that you are being a godly wife is the only reason you are still alive, breathing, and not struggling with sickness. Maybe the fact that you are being a Godly husband is the only reason your children are blessed and doing well. The fact is God cannot lie and His word cannot fail. If you do right by God, He will do right by you. The Bible says you will reap what you sow. The Bible says, "I have never seen the righteous forsaken." The Bible says that God is not slack concerning His promises. The Bible says the joy of the Lord is my strength. There are so many verses that talk about God's provision, protection, love, and joy He gives us.

Maybe you are wasting all of your time and energy trying to change somebody. You keep on preaching to them, arguing with them, and trying to do everything you can do to save or fix them. You get so focused on changing them that they become an idol to you and you neglect your time with God. They start stressing you out so badly and you don't have the energy to do the things that God has asked of you. You forsake your individual responsibilities that we talked about at the start of this book trying to fight your own battles and fix your spouse's. You end up sacrificing your relationship, your ministry, and what God has called you to do by dealing with a distraction from the enemy. This is why the Bible says obedience is better than sacrifice. You can sit there and say, "Lord, look at everything I gave up dealing with this person," but, on the other hand, God is like, "But it dwindled your prayer life." You spent all your time chasing after your husband or catering toward your wife that you lost your relationship with God. You wonder why you are not seeing a return for all of your sacrifice? It is because you stopped being obedient. You didn't trust God enough to put it in His hands and maintain your balance.

We have to be careful that we don't become imbalanced spiritually. The way you do this is by keeping your faith. No matter what everybody else is doing, maintain your relationship, your walk with God, and your obedience to God. If you are the only one being a peacemaker in the house, don't stop. If you are the only one loving in the house, don't stop. Just know that there comes a time where you must shake the dust from your feet and let God be God and trust Him and His word.

We don't have the power to change or save somebody. We don't have the power to put someone in heaven or hell. We should always focus on showing our spouse the love of Christ regardless of what things look like. It is the Word of God and the power of His love that will transform, convict, and change them. We have to have the faith in God to release it from our hands and allow God to do what needs to be done.

It may not always feel like everything is going the best. It may not even feel like God is aware of what is going on in your marriage and life. Just know that God sees everything, and even if it does not feel like it's working, God is working it, but it is probably not in line with your time frame. The victory is not going to come the way you expected, but if you stick to the blueprint found in the word of God, everything will work out just fine. You must endure, be faithful, be obedient, and keep on fighting for your marriage. The devil would love to get you to quit. He would love to see you fail. He would love for you to stop at the test and never get to the testimony. He does not want you to overcome and have a blessed marriage because that is what God desires for you to have. Whatever God has for you, the enemy is going to try to steal it.

At the end of the day, you need to realize that the enemy can only have your marriage if you let him. Have you prayed about your marriage as much as you have complained? Have you gotten up out of bed and sacrificed sleep or gone on a fast to fight for your marriage in the Spirit? Sometimes, God wants to see how much fight you have in you. He wants to see faith alive in you through your actions and choices. If you know God hates divorce, and you call yourself a follower of God, you've got to put everything you can into making your marriage work because that is what God would want for you. Once you can sit down and look in the mirror at your I dos and your I don'ts and be able to say, "I gave it all to God," that is when God will take over. Marriage is your first ministry before anything else. God will not expand your ministry or anointing if you don't give your all into your marriage.

If you follow the steps in this book, pull out your Bible, and see what else it has to say about marriage before you actually get married, I promise you will save yourself so much heartache. If you read this book and are already married and you've realized you didn't build your marriage on the proper foundation, it is okay. It is always possible to do some repairs. No matter what stage you are at, if you follow the blueprint found in God's word and those principles over your feelings, you will have a blessed, passionate, and victorious marriage.

There are somethings in this book that you will not want to do and there are other things you wish your spouse would do. Sometimes, you need to take the focus off what you want and what you won't do, and put the focus on what your spouse wants and say, "I will, I do, because I love you."

I know some things in this book and in the Bible may seem like it is too much to carry. Just understand that it will require some large sacrifice on you and your partner. If you are not familiar with sacrifice, you are not familiar with love. If you are not familiar with love, you are not familiar with God. God is love embodied, and He tells us in scripture that people will know we are His by the way we love one another.

True love and sacrifice walk hand in hand. Just learn to respect your spouse and submit to the word of God. Make up your mind to say, "I do," to the things God requires of you and, "I don't," to the things that will damage your marriage. I pray that God blesses your marriage and gives you the strength you need to fight back against everything that tries to rip you two apart!

BEFORE YOU JUMP

efore you jump into a marriage, here are a few questions to ask yourself. It is so easy to blindly follow our feelings, but use these questions to get out of your feelings, and actually put some thought into the direction you are going.

For Men

1) Does she have her own personal healthy relationship with God?
2) Has that relationship been consistent?
3) Does she have some kind of accountability in her life?
4) How is her relationship with her father? If he wasn't there has she healed from father wounds?
5) How are the woman in her life? Are they married? Are they baby mamas? Are they single and bitter? Are they men jumpers?
6) Does she have goals that she is pursuing something in this life?
7) Does she bring anything to the table other than sex?
8) When you have an argument how does she carry herself?
9) Is she thirsty for attention from men and through social media?
10) Read Proverbs 31, does she line up with some of that?
11) Has she been raped or molested in her lifetime? How many sexual partners has she had? Has she healed from these wounds? (Healing is important when it comes to these things)

12) Does she try to control or manipulate you with threats, emotions, are other guys?

13) How long ago was her last relationship? Are you the rebound?

14) Was she with somebody else when you started talking to her?

15) If she has kids, what kind of mother is she?

16) Did she have sex with you right away if you were in sin when you met?

17) Are you saving her from a bad situation?

18) Is it lust or love?

19) Does she build you up and support who you are as a man and who you want to be? Or, does she only tear you down?

20) Can you live without her?

21) Do you trust her with your heart, life, home, and dreams?

22) Does she compliment or contradict what God is trying to do in your life?

23) Do you still have interest in another woman, or is she the only one you are into?

24) Is her emotional wellbeing consistent or erratic?

25) How does she get along with your family?

Ladies want to know is he the one?

1) Is he leading you closer to God?

2) Does he have a job?

3) Does he have a church home with a Pastor?

4) Does he have accountability in his life?

5) How is his relationship with his father?

6) How does he treat his sisters and mother?

7) Does he struggle with insecurity because of past women who hurt him?

8) Does he trust you?

9) Does he love you like Christ loves the church?

10) Does he lead you into prayer or into his sheets? Where is he leading you? Destiny, purpose, life?

11) Does he make you want more of God?
12) Does he isolate himself from any type of brotherhood or leadership in his life?
13) Does he pay his tithes, bills, and offering?
14) Is he is easily angered or offended?
15) If he has kids, does he take care of them? Does he respect the mother of his kids?
16) Do you compliment one another's destiny in Christ? Is it a good fit?
17) Did he cheat on someone to get with you?
18) Is he lazy?
19) Does he make an effort to show you he cares?
20) Does he think he is God's gift to women?
21) Do you feel safe with him?
22) Was he ever molested or raped?
23) Do you see Jesus reflected in him?
24) Do you see the fruits of the Spirit when he interacts with you and others?
25) Why are you with him?
26) Did you manipulate him, or lie to him to get him?
27) Are you still thinking about your ex when you are with him?
28) Can he lead, provide, and protect his family?
29) Does he listen to you?
30) Does he have a prayer life?

Why Should We Listen to You

It is funny to me how when we want something to be from God, we take anything as a sign from God. You want to be with a person so bad, you take everything as a sign from God. Listen, just because you guys look good together doesn't mean you're good together. It looks nice on Snapchat, IG, and FB; but, spiritually, it's not always a good fit. He's tall, you fine, that don't mean it's meant to be. He's rich, you're poor, doesn't mean it's sent from God. He got three kids, you got four kids that equals seven, and seven means complete, doesn't mean it's sent from God. You pay eight hundred in child support, her baby daddy pay her eight hundred in child support, doesn't mean God just made a way of escape for you. You like pizza, she likes pizza, doesn't mean it's sent from God. You both been divorced, doesn't mean it's from God. He said praise the Lord to you in the parking lot doesn't mean he is the one. She made eye contact with you when she was singing on the praise team, and you was in the front row, doesn't mean it's from God. You should have had your eyes on Jesus. You white, and she white; you black, and she black doesn't mean it's sent from God. What God has for you might not make sense to you or other people, so I want you to trust Him. If you know anything about me, the first thing you might be thinking is "why should I listen to you, of all people?" I will tell you Paul and many others in the Bible spoke on marriage through inspiration of the Holy Spirit without being married, or even with having marriage issues. Follow me, and I promise you will see.

I want to challenge your perspective on your marriage and marriage as a definition as you begin to read this book. I often times see that one of the biggest ways the enemy has destroyed dreams, hope, faith, marriages, and families is by feeding them a false perspective. If people saw their marriage the way that God does, I believe they would have more motivation, desire, and compassion to make their marriage the best union it could be. We live in a world where people simply throw in the towel when their marriage is not giving them what they want instead of planting seed into their marriage in hopes that it would grow. I want you to read through this book and evaluate not only your marriage as a whole, but your individual contribution to your marriage and how that affects it.

What is the purpose of your marriage? Why are you married to your spouse? Is there more to your marriage that you have not explored? How does your marriage line up with other marriages around you? Does your marriage feel like a partnership, a team effort, slavery, a burden, a dead end, or something that is continually evolving every day? Does the person you are thinking about marrying fit the direction God is trying to take you? Will they contribute to the foundation, or challenge and hinder everything you try to build?

Marriage is one of the most beautiful things that God created. We often run into problems in our marriage because we are not following the blueprint for successful building found in the word of God. Everybody has a unique journey, but the word of God applies to us all in the same way. If you learn how to do marriage, and be a husband or a wife Gods way, you will have a blessed and victorious life.

God has bigger plans for your marriage than just being with that one person for the rest of your life. There are so many books that try to show us how to have a good marriage, but the truth of the matter is everything you need to know can be found in the Bible. If you build off of the foundation found in the word of God, not only will your marriage withstand the storm and stand tall, but it will be a beautiful sight and inspiration to others.

I am open and honest with my life. Anybody can go online and see many of my trials and testimonies. It is no secret that I got married at nineteen and went off to Iraq seven months later. It is no secret that that marriage ended with me filing for divorce. I got married for the wrong reasons, and I didn't do things God's way. I never had a father in my life to teach me certain things that a man should know. I went about all the wrong ways trying to fix my marriage, fulfill my needs, and change my wife. I take full responsibility for that marriage being destroyed by the enemy. I wasn't ready to be a husband and I had a lot to learn. In marriage, it always takes two to tango, but I also realize that God has a unique relationship with the man and woman. There are God-given requirements to being a man or woman in the Bible. I want to start off this book by showing you what God requires of you individually as a person, then go deeper and show you what He requires of you as a husband or a wife.

I was recently in my second marriage, and I took a completely different approach. I went to a lot of counseling and so did my wife. I read a lot of books, asked many older couples for advice, but the biggest thing that helped me fight for that marriage was falling before the face of God and asking Him for directions. That marriage was even harder in its earlier days than my first one was. I have gone through almost everything you can imagine.

One thing I've learned is that you must realize that your spouse is not the enemy, and sometimes there are deeper issues underneath the surface of what we see. You may look at what is in front of you and get offended or upset, but fail to realize that what you are looking at is not a true reflection of who your spouse is. It reflects the hurt or attack going on inside of them.

Many of you know I have been married twice, and neither one of those marriages worked. You also may know that I grew up without a father, and I never knew how to be a man or what it means to be a husband. It would seem like knowing all of these things about me would disqualify me from even touching this subject with a ten-foot pole. The reality is that I wrote most of this book while I was fighting for my second marriage and going through the transition of divorce. I studied, I prayed, I sought counseling, and I learned so many things that gave me a serious wake up call. If I had known in my early twenties what I know now at thirty-one, no discredit to my ex-wives, but we would have never gotten married. Life is a great teacher, and sometimes, we learn things the hard way. I have realized that I didn't even know who I was as a man until I was about twenty-seven. Everything I did before that was based off of following my feelings, and nobody ever taught me that that is the worst thing you can do.

You may think, *Why should I listen to anything you have to say?* Well, instead of me being bitter, I choose to share everything I had to learn the hard way. I hope to help young people avoid making the same mistakes. I also want people to know that even though in my marriages we were completely unequally yoked and outside of God's will, we found ways to make it work through trial and error as long as we could. The end result being that we simply did not have the same belief system, and my sold out to Jesus lifestyle was not matching the one she wanted for herself. If you spoke to either one of my exes, they will tell you the same thing, we tried to make something work that God was never involved in. Legalistic people will bash, and judge, but God taught me that there is grace and mercy for our mistakes. People come from all kinds of different backgrounds and situations. It is foolish to judge somebody for where they are, when you don't know where they started. People will often try to judge you by what you been through, thinking they would never be in your situation, but the reality is they never had to face the things you faced. The only perfect one is God. If you have a story like mine, don't be discouraged and lose hope because of legalistic people. If you repent and seek wisdom, God will turn your life around and give you a clean start!

No marriage is perfect. Some may be better or worse than others, but the grass is never greener on the other side in God's economy. What I mean by that is that God wants your marriage to survive and thrive. It is never His will for divorce. If you are with someone who is willing to make the marriage work, you two can overcome everything. Unfortunately, that was not the case in my marriage, and the direction God was taking me was not one my ex-wife was willing to go. We simply did not share the same belief system. I will touch on that later in this book.

I feel like sometimes because we follow our own lust, and we don't know any better, we often get into situations that God never intended for us. Because of that, grace is granted to those who do get a divorce. But, the reality is that when you follow God's word, you can never go wrong. Some people don't have the knowledge of truth, and God must clean up the messes we make. Repent and move forward in Jesus name once you come to truth. I don't want you to get discouraged by legalistic Christians either. I will address these topics in this book, and hopefully you will get come clarity and peace of mind.

Just know that God wants your marriage to succeed and be great! When you follow God's will, you will always be blessed, and nobody can bless you like God can. The world is quick to divorce and get remarried, and it may seem like they found greener grass, but that is what you see in the carnal. It is a completely different thing when you see it in the spiritual from Gods perspective. God does not look at your marriage the way the world has come to look at marriage. God does not even look at your spouse the way you look at them. You want to get to the point in your walk with God and your marriage where you are seeing things the way that God sees them and you are moving under the influence of His direction and Spirit.

The grass may look greener on the other side, but that is because somebody watered it. Your best friend may look like she got a better husband than you, but what if she is happy and her husband isn't? What if he treats her completely different when they get behind closed doors? What if he is treating her better than your husband treats you because she respects and honors her husband in ways that you don't yours? Your homeboy may seem like his wife is just so much better than yours. Maybe she looks prettier and is in better shape than your wife. Maybe he gets more sex and respect than you. Maybe his wife submits and keeps the house clean. But, what if she is treating him better than your wife treats you because he waters the grass? What if your wife is not a lot of things, but she is faithful, and his wife is cheating behind his back and you never know it? What if she is in shape, but she is always talking down on her husband behind closed doors?

I say this to say that you never know what is really going on in someone else's marriage. You may envy the greener grass you see, but are you willing to do the work it took to get that grass so green? Are you willing to pull the weeds, cut the grass, chase off the critters, and make sure the grass is getting the proper sunlight? Marriage takes work. A lot of people like the idea of marriage, but find out they don't like the work and sacrifice that it takes to keep one going. If you are a selfish person, you are not ready to be married because marriage is about serving one another. Marriage is about giving yourself to someone else even if you don't always feel like it.

There are many marriages that are just barely surviving and not thriving. Usually, this is because one person is giving more than the other. You may be that spouse that is the glue that is holding your marriage and your family together. You may feel like everything in the world is trying to destroy your marriage, but you keep on fighting for it. I know it can be very hard not to be bitter. I know it can be very hard to lose hope, but I want you to trust that God can turn it around.

Maybe you are reading this book with your spouse, and both of you have given up. Maybe you have come to the conclusion that you guys just don't fit together and have no chemistry. I want you to rebuke those lies today and get a fresh perspective. The greatest thing you have in common is that you both were created by a loving God, and if you would submit your marriage to Him, He in turn can give your marriage a miracle. God is the creator of the universe. He created the sun, the stars, the moon, and He can create chemistry, love, and passion in your marriage.

I want you to read this book and see what the *I dos and I don'ts* of your marriage are. I want you to read this book and have a mental picture of the balance of your marriage. I want you to understand that through Jesus Christ, you have the power to move things around on that scale and tip your marriage from disaster to beautiful success today!

I have been through nearly everything bad I can think of that a marriage can go through. I have seen my marriage slipping through my fingers feeling helpless. I have been the problem in the marriage, and I have been the only one holding it together. Through all the trials, pain, tears, and failure, I fell on my face before God and sought Him like never before. I learned that most of the time the reason we have marriage problems and a high divorce rate is because we are simply doing marriage wrong. We are looking at our marriage with the wrong perspective. We are getting married for the wrong reasons. We are not honoring our vows and what they mean. We take divorce as a normal way of life. We don't fully comprehend the significance of marrying a person. We don't even know how to be husbands or wives because nobody showed us, or what they did show us was wrong. We come into marriage with a "what can they do for me?" attitude as opposed to a "what can I do for them and what can we accomplish together?" attitude.

You need to understand that your marriage is a team effort. When your partner is going through a rough season, they shouldn't feel alone. You need to have the mentality that what is yours is theirs and what is theirs is yours. If the enemy is coming against you, he is coming against the both of you. You may not always have the right words to say, and sometimes there will really be nothing you can do about certain situations, but let your spouse know you have their back. Let them know everything is going to be okay and pray for them through those bad times. God will accomplish more through your prayers than anything else you do. With every chapter you read in this book, I want you to do away with thinking "they" all the time. Stop thinking they have a problem, they messed up, they have the issue, they are the screw up, and look at your marriage and every-thing that comes with it or affects it as an "us" thing. Too many times, couples point fingers instead of extending hands of support, love and encouragement. I want you to go to your spouse today, look them in the eye and say "we are in this together, I choose to navigate, experience, and figure out this life with you!"

I am here to challenge the way you see marriage in general, and hopefully change your perspective for the better on how you see yours. I want to show you how to build a marriage on the right foundation and avoid learning some lessons that you could avoid if somebody had just taken the time to show you the way. I want you to have clear direction and hope for your current or future marriage. The best days of your marriage are ahead of you. Allow me to give you something to compliment your journey. I wrote this book in a way as if we are building a foundation. I want to lead you the way the Lord led me, and I know this will bless your life and marriage and save you so much trouble if you apply it.

ABOUT THE AUTHOR

Marcus J Rogers was born in Weisbaden, Germany, on July 19, 1986. He started following the Lord at the age of seven. He was homeschooled and went to college for one year before joining the Army at eighteen. He has been in the military for thirteen years and is currently making his way out of the military and pursuing full time ministry.

He has two combat deployments to Iraq and Afghanistan and one tour in South Korea. During his tours, he drew closer to God and found out the calling on his life. God gave him visions of worldwide revival and a great army rising up in the last days that would be bold and on fire for God. The Lord sent him out to set God's people on fire and to preach the message of repentance. As he continued to do street preaching and posting videos on social media, doors started opening for him. He is the author of *Through the Fire to Be on Fire*, and he is currently working on a few other books. His long-term goal is to open a church on the north side of Chicago called Firehouse, his short-term goals are to take the gospel to the streets, feed the homeless, and preach revivals across the nation.

His favorite quote is, "I am just a nobody, trying to tell everybody about somebody who can save anybody."

CPSIA information can be obtained
at www.ICGtesting.com
Printed in the USA
LVHW090209110519
617518LV00001B/147/P